Getting Started
with
Structured BASIC

Wiley PC Companions

Stern/Stern: GETTING STARTED WITH STRUCTURED BASIC, Second Edition
Murphy: GETTING STARTED WITH DOS 5.0
Russakoff: GETTING STARTED WITH WINDOWS 3.1
Kronstadt/Sachs: DISCOVERING MICROSOFT WORKS 2.0
Murphy: GETTING STARTED WITH WORDPERFECT 4.2/5.0**
Murphy: GETTING STARTED WITH WORDPERFECT 5.1
Murphy/Potter: GETTING STARTED WITH LOTUS 1-2-3, RELEASE 2.2
Farrell: GETTING STARTED WITH LOTUS 1-2-3, RELEASE 2.3
Murphy: GETTING STARTED WITH QUATTRO**
Arnolds/Hammonds/Isham: GETTING STARTED WITH dBASE III PLUS**
Gaylord: GETTING STARTED WITH dBASE IV
Wiley: EXPLORING DOS, WORDPERFECT 5.1, LOTUS 1-2-3 (RELEASE 2.2), AND dBASE
    III PLUS

** Educational version software available

Wiley Macintosh Companions

Abernethy, Nanney and Porter: EXPLORING MACINTOSH: Concepts in Visually Oriented
    Computing
Nanney, Porter and Abernethy: EXPLORING MICROSOFT WORKS 2.0—Macintosh

Getting Started with Structured BASIC

Second Edition

Nancy Stern
Hofstra University

Robert A. Stern
Nassau Community College

John Wiley & Sons, Inc.
New York   Chichester   Brisbane   Toronto   Singapore

ACQUISITIONS EDITOR   Beth Lang Golub
MARKETING MANAGER   Carolyn Henderson
PRODUCTION SUPERVISOR   Charlotte Hyland
MANUFACTURING MANAGER   Andrea Price
COPY EDITING SUPERVISOR   Deborah Herbert

This book was set in Garamond Light by GTS Graphics and printed and bound by Hamilton Printing. The cover was printed by Lehigh Press.

ISBN 0-471-58709-5

Printed in the United States of America

10 9 8 7 6 5 4 3 2 1

To Melanie and Lori

PREFACE

This book, which is part of the Wiley *Getting Started* series on software tutorials, focuses on structured BASIC programming for IBM PCs and their compatibles. The book can be used as a self-teaching guide or as a tutorial in conjunction with (1) an introductory course in computing, or (2) a BASIC programming course. No prior programming or computing experience is needed.

This book covers the fundamentals of BASIC programming, not the advanced features of the language. The syntax explained in the text is compatible with virtually every PC version of BASIC; where there are fundamental differences, they are specifically addressed in the text. In addition, the programming concepts described in the text are common to all versions of BASIC and, indeed, to all programming languages. We use pseudocode throughout the book as a program planning tool. We have written a relatively short introduction to BASIC that will enable students to write elementary- and intermediate-level programs in a relatively short time.

This book includes many of the pedagogic tools common to our other computing texts. Each chapter is in outline form and has a step-by-step presentation of material followed by numerous examples. Most chapters have self-tests with solutions at key points within the chapter, full chapter self-tests, and review questions that can be assigned for homework.

Many BASIC books claim to present a structured version of the language but actually begin with nonstructured examples or with a focus on syntax that fails to address structured programming concepts. From the very onset, we focus on BASIC programs that handle a variable amount of input and that are fully structured.

In addition to emphasizing structured concepts, we focus on other programming techniques for making programs easier to read, debug, maintain, and modify. These include top-down and modular programming concepts and stylistic features such as useful naming conventions and conventions for displaying meaningful comments.

We thank the following people at John Wiley for their assistance and support in the preparation of this book:

Editorial—Beth Lang Golub, Bill Oldsey, Bonnie Lieberman
Production—Charlotte Hyland, Lucille Buonocore, Ann Berlin
Marketing—Carolyn Henderson, Steve Kraham
Proofreading—Shelley Flannery, Suzanne Ingrao
Copy Editing—Mary Konstant

We thank the following people for their assistance in reviewing the manuscript:

Gary Baker
Marshalltown Community College

Virginia Gregory
Hofstra University

Marilyn Meyer
Fresno City College

Bill Smith
Nassau Community College

Floyd Winters
Manatee Community College

Finally, we express our appreciation to our assistant, Carol L. Eisen, for her assistance in preparing the manuscript.

If you have any questions, comments, or suggestions regarding this book, please contact us through our editor, Beth Lang Golub, at John Wiley and Sons, Inc., 605 Third Avenue, New York, NY 10158, 212-850-8619. We can also be reached via Bitnet at ACSNNS@HOFSTRA, or via Internet at ACSNNS@VAXC.HOFSTRA.EDU.

Nancy Stern
Robert A. Stern

CONTENTS

1

The Nature of BASIC

BASIC as a Universal Language

BASIC is designed to be an easy-to-learn programming language that you can use for writing programs in many applications areas. The term *BASIC* is an acronym for *B*eginner's *A*ll-Purpose *S*ymbolic *I*nstruction *C*ode. When it was developed in the early 1960s by John Kemeny and Thomas Kurtz at Dartmouth College, BASIC was one of only a few existing symbolic programming languages. It gained immediate and widespread popularity because it is easy to learn, easy to use and, at the same time, powerful and flexible.

Today, there are dozens if not hundreds of versions of BASIC available for microcomputers as well as mainframes. In fact, when micros were introduced in the 1970s, BASIC was the first and, in most instances, the only symbolic programming language available for them. It remains the most widely used symbolic language for microcomputers, and it is still used on mainframes as well.

Most Commonly Used Versions for Micros

Although there are numerous versions of BASIC for micros, several are predominant in the current marketplace. Note that PC-DOS is the version of DOS for IBM personal computers (PCs), and MS-DOS is a comparable version for IBM-compatible PCs.

Most Common Versions of BASIC for IBM PCs and IBM-Compatible PCs

Name	How to Acquire	Features
QBASIC	Comes with PC-DOS 5 and higher	Can be used on IBM PCs and IBM-compatible PCs
BASICA	Comes with PC-DOS 4 and lower	Can be used only on IBM computers and *some* compatibles
QuickBASIC	Developed and sold by Microsoft for under $100	Can be used on IBM PCs and IBM-compatible PCs

1

GW-BASIC	Used with MS-DOS, most often bundled with it; can be purchased for under $100	An older version of BASIC for IBM-compatible PCs; similar to BASICA for IBM computers
BASIC	Comes with PC-DOS 4 and lower	Very limited version just for IBM PCs

Most inexpensive versions of BASIC—like those just mentioned—are interpreted, not compiled. Only QuickBASIC, the most advanced of the BASIC versions discussed in this text, gives you an option of either compiling or interpreting your program.

Compiled versions of a language save the translated, machine language code in a program file that can then be executed over and over again. Because the need for repeated translations is eliminated, compiled versions of BASIC are more useful for programs that are to be run repeatedly than are interpreted versions, which must be retranslated before each program run. For example, programs to be run on a regular production basis are typically compiled. In addition, compiled versions of BASIC tend to translate and run faster. Most compiled versions of BASIC, like QuickBASIC, are fully compatible with QBASIC and BASICA. This means that programs written in QBASIC or BASICA can be translated into QuickBASIC and then executed with little or no modification by means of QuickBASIC compilers.

QBASIC (for PC-DOS and MS-DOS 5.0 and higher) and BASICA (for PC-DOS 4 and lower on IBM computers) are typically bundled with the DOS disks themselves so that their actual cost is negligible. As a result, they have been the most widely used versions for IBM micros and their compatibles. QBASIC will likely become as popular in the years ahead because it is bundled with all newer versions of DOS.

Compiled versions of BASIC, including QuickBASIC, must be purchased separately, but they typically sell for under $100.

QBASIC is significantly more advanced than BASICA and has a menu format that is more user-friendly. In this text we consider both QBASIC and BASICA in detail and highlight their differences. We discuss the even more advanced QuickBASIC as well. As noted, BASICA programs can easily be converted to QBASIC or QuickBASIC format later on.

We focus on a common core of QBASIC and BASICA instructions that are likely to run, with perhaps minor adjustments, using any version of BASIC.

To load in a version of BASIC, type the program name (QBASIC, BASICA, QB, and so on) and press the Enter key. You are then ready to enter a program.

With QBASIC, a full-screen display appears after you type QBASIC. See Figure 1.1. Press the Esc key to clear the welcome message so that you can begin entering a program.

With BASICA, prompts appear as in Figure 1.2 when you type the BASICA command. With BASICA, you can begin typing a program immediately.

Steps Involved in Writing Programs

Before discussing QBASIC and BASICA in depth, let us review the steps involved in writing programs and the techniques that should be used for creating well-designed programs.

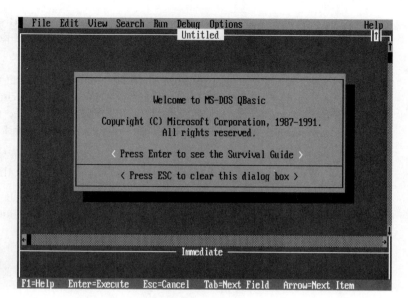

Figure 1.1
Initial QBASIC screen.

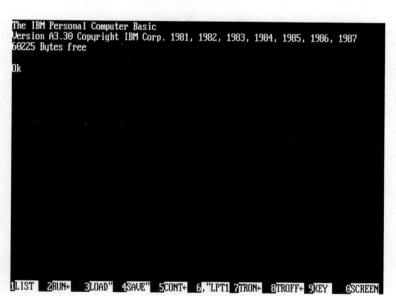

Figure 1.2
Initial BASICA screen.

1. Obtain the program requirements and specifications from a systems analyst or from the user. A programmer can interact with either, depending on the organization.

2. Plan the program using standard planning tools such as pseudocode and hierarchy charts.

3. Write the program and desk-check it before keying it in.

4. Key in the program and desk-check it again; watch out for typos.

5. Translate the program by means of either a BASIC compiler or interpreter. If

there are any rule violations or syntax errors, they will be displayed on the screen. Fix them and retranslate the program until there are no more syntax errors.

6. Run the program using test data that includes a sample of what the actual data is likely to look like. Using pencil and paper, manually determine the results you should get and compare them with the computer-produced results. If there are discrepancies, find the errors, fix them, and retranslate and rerun the program until all the results are correct.

7. Test the program with actual data to ensure that it runs smoothly in a normal operating environment.

8. Document the program so that users can run it without your intervention.

2

Techniques for Good Program Design

Before you begin to write actual programs in the BASIC language, take the time to review the following fundamental techniques for good program design.

Structured Programming

The most important technique for coding well-designed programs is called **structured programming.** Structured programming standardizes program design so that all programs, regardless of the language in which they are written, have a similar form. In general, structured programs are easier to read than nonstructured programs. They are also easier to debug and modify if changes are required at a later date. Moreover, they are easier to evaluate: programming managers and systems analysts are better able to assess programmers' skills and the quality of their programs.

For those of you who have had some previous programming experience, you may have encountered nonstructured techniques such as the frequent use of GOTOs, which is another term for a branch instruction. One major purpose of structured programming is to simplify debugging by reducing the number of entry and exit points (or "GOTOs") in a program. For that reason, structured programming is sometimes referred to as GOTO-less programming. Through the techniques of structured programming, the GOTO statement is avoided entirely. In BASIC, this means writing programs in which sequences are controlled by WHILE loops or some other logical control statement.

Modular Programming

Long and complex structured programs are sometimes subdivided into **modules**—also called **subroutines,** subprograms, or procedures. These are separate sets of instructions that accomplish distinct functions. Programs that are subdivided into modules are called modular programs; that is, subroutines, subprograms, or procedures are written as separate sections and are called into the main body of a program when they are needed.

5

Program modules are not only written separately, but they also are often tested independently. This makes it possible to segment a large or complex program into individual sections so that, if necessary, different programmers can code and debug these different sections. In summary, modular programs consist of individual sections that are executed under the control of a main module.

Top-Down Programming

Another important design technique that makes programs easier to read and more efficient is called **top-down programming.** Top-down programming implies that proper program design is best achieved by designing and coding major modules before minor ones. Thus, in a top-down program, the main modules are coded first, then intermediate modules are coded, and finally the minor ones are coded. By coding modules in this top-down manner, the organization or flow of the program is given primary attention.

The standardized top-down technique provides an effective complement to structured programming, thereby achieving efficient and effective program design.

In this text we use structured techniques in all our programs and avoid GOTOs entirely. In addition, we use a top-down approach in the more advanced programs so that you will learn to program in a manner that is widely accepted as a standard one.

3

A Sample BASIC Program

To understand the nature of BASIC, we will first look at a sample program that solves a typical business problem. This program will run with all versions of the BASIC language.

Definition of the Problem

A computer center of a company is assigned the task of calculating weekly wages (gross pay) for all nonsalaried personnel. The employee name, hourly rate, and number of hours worked are supplied as input for each employee, and the weekly wages figure is to be computed as follows:

$$\text{Weekly Wages} = \text{Hours Worked} \times \text{Hourly Rate}$$

Before processing can begin, the incoming data or input must be in a form that is "readable" by the computer. The input may be keyed in or read in from a disk or other storage medium.

Input Layout

Let us assume that the employee data will be keyed by means of a keyboard. As you will see later, the device used for entering the input does not really affect the program's logic.

Each employee's data consists of three fields called **variables**. A variable is a storage area that will contain data. We will name the three variables that will contain inputted data EMPNAME\$, HOURS, and RATE. Later, when we discuss rules for forming variable names, you will see that the \$ in EMPNAME\$ is required when you are defining a variable that can contain alphabetic data.

Output Layout and Definition

For each EMPNAME\$, HOURS, and RATE entered on the keyboard, the computer will display on a screen the employee's name and his or her weekly WAGES, which will be calculated as HOURS multiplied by RATE.

7

The Program Illustrated

To examine the program in detail, we will first look at its specifications, then the coding guidelines, and finally the instructions themselves.

The Program Specifications

Recall that the program development process begins when the programmer obtains the program specifications. The program specifications for this problem include the formats of both the input and output and a description of the processing to be performed. This has already been provided in the previous section.

Once these specifications have been supplied, the programmer plans the program's design. This means mapping out the logic to be used in the program. The following pseudocode describes the logic to be used in the sample program. We include pseudocode as a planning tool here because we think you should become familiar with reading pseudocode before actually preparing it. The basic rules for writing pseudocode are provided in the next section.

```
START
        Print a message to user describing the input to be entered
        Input EMPNAME$, HOURS, and RATE
        WHILE there is still input
                Calculate WAGES as HOURS × RATE
                Display the results
                Input EMPNAME$, HOURS, and RATE
        WEND
        Print a message indicating End of Report
STOP
```

After the program has been planned using pseudocode or another planning tool, the programmer is ready to code it. Recall that a program is a set of instructions that operate on input to produce output. Consider the following simplified QBASIC and BASICA programs that input employee data keyed in using a keyboard and display a line containing the computed wages for each employee along with the employee's name:

• QBASIC (or QuickBASIC)

```
'This Program Calculates Weekly Wages
PRINT "Enter Name, Hours and Rate"
INPUT EMPNAME$, HOURS, RATE
WHILE HOURS < 999
        LET WAGES = HOURS * RATE
        PRINT "Weekly Wages for "; EMPNAME$; " is "; WAGES
        INPUT EMPNAME$, HOURS, RATE
WEND
PRINT "End of Report"
END
```

The same program but with line numbers appears next.

- **BASICA or GW-BASIC**

```
10   ' This Program Calculates Weekly Wages
20   PRINT "Enter Name, Hours and Rate"
30   INPUT EMPNAME$, HOURS, RATE
40   WHILE HOURS < 999
50       LET WAGES = HOURS * RATE
60       PRINT "Weekly Wages for "; EMPNAME$; " is "; WAGES
70       INPUT EMPNAME$, HOURS, RATE
80   WEND
90   PRINT "End of Report"
100  END
```

The numbers 10 through 100 on the left in the BASICA program are line numbers. As we will see, BASICA programs are executed in line number sequence. QBASIC programs are executed in the sequence displayed so they do not need line numbers. In fact, we recommend that you do *not* use line numbers with QBASIC because they have no real meaning.

Both programs are likely to be executable, as is, with most versions of BASIC. At worst, minor modifications might be necessary. Remember, the programs are identical except for the line numbers, which are required with BASICA but, as stated previously, are optional with QBASIC.

Figure 3.1 shows this program as we entered it using QBASIC.

This sample program can operate on any number of inputted values. Business programs typically operate on numerous data items, and the number of these items is usually unknown when the program is written. Moreover, if a program is run periodically, the number of inputted data items often changes. For example, the

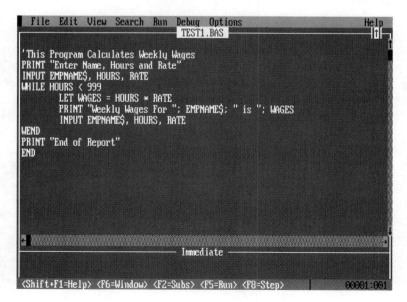

Figure 3.1
Sample program entered using QBASIC.

number of employees can be 100 in one week, 98 the next week, 103 the third week, and so on. Consequently, most business programs use a WHILE **loop**, like the one illustrated, to specify repeated execution of a series of steps. In this instance, WHILE there is still valid data to process, the program continues to do so. WHILE . . . WEND in the program delimits, or sets the limit of, the loop. Some versions of BASIC use WHILE . . . LOOP (VAX), WHILE . . . NEXT, DO . . . LOOP, and so on in place of WHILE . . . WEND. Even though the actual words or syntax may vary slightly, the important thing to remember is that the instructions within the WHILE loop are executed repeatedly until there is no more data to process.

Coding Guidelines

Each line in a BASICA program must have a line number, but these are optional for QBASIC and most other versions. For BASICA, you should use multiples of 10 in line numbering (10, 20, etc.) so that you can easily make insertions if the need arises. If you need to add a line between lines 20 and 30, for example, you can number it as line 25. Note, however, that with BASICA, instructions are executed in line number sequence, *regardless* of how they are entered. If you accidentally code:

```
10
30
20
```

the instructions will be executed as follows:

QBASIC
In the sequence entered:
10, 30, 20—the line numbers have no meaning

BASICA
In line number sequence:
10, 20, 30

This is an important difference between QBASIC and BASICA. Line numbers determine the sequence of instructions executed in BASICA but have no impact on sequence in QBASIC. We again encourage you to omit them for QBASIC.

As a matter of style, we capitalize all BASIC key words such as PRINT, INPUT, and WHILE, as well as variables such as EMPNAME$, HOURS, and RATE. This is a *convention* but is not a *requirement*. BASIC is a case-insensitive language, which means that the translator ignores the distinction between uppercase and lowercase letters. PRINT, print, Print, or even PRInt, for example, are all interpreted as the same word. Some versions of BASIC, such as QBASIC and BASICA, automatically convert key words that are part of instructions to uppercase; BASICA also converts the names of variables to uppercase.

Instructions

Each instruction in a BASIC program is executed in sequence unless a logical control construct like the WHILE is performed.

Let us consider each instruction of the sample program in sequence. The first line in the program is:

```
' This Program Calculates Weekly Wages
```

This line is a comment line; that means it is coded just for information purposes and has no effect on either the translation or execution of the program. Comment lines begin with a ' (apostrophe or single quote) or with the abbreviation REM for REMARK. Once a ' or REM is sensed on any line, the rest of the line is treated as a comment and is not translated or executed in the program. Any instruction line can have a comment as its only entry, or an instruction can have a comment added to it. For example, the following END instruction includes a comment that is not compiled or executed:

```
END   REM This is the last line of a program
```

or

```
END   'This is the last line of a program
```

Use comments freely in your programs because they help others understand your coding and logic. They may even remind you of some details later when you are testing the program.

The second line in the program is:

```
PRINT "Enter Name, Hours and Rate"
```

This line, when executed or run, will display a message on the screen to the user. It is intended to help the user determine the input to be entered and the form that the input should take. In a PRINT statement, the words between the double quotation marks are displayed on the screen as is. When the program is executed, these words appear on the screen where input and output are displayed.

When keying in double quotes to delimit the beginning of the message and the end of the message in a PRINT statement, use the keyboard's symbol for double quotes ("). This symbol is the same for open quote and close quote.

The message in the PRINT instruction is called a **literal** or **string constant**. Do not confuse this PRINT instruction with a comment line. A comment appears within the program itself only as a remark to the programmer. A PRINT instruction, when executed, prints a message to the user at the time the program is run.

Consider the next instruction in our sample program:

```
INPUT EMPNAME$, HOURS, RATE
```

This INPUT instruction accepts three values to be entered by the user on the keyboard. When the INPUT instruction is executed, the computer prints a ? on the screen. The ? is called a **prompt** because it signals the user that the computer is waiting for input to be entered. In this case, three values must be keyed in by the user, each separated by a comma. After the three values have been entered, the user must press the Enter key on the keyboard to transmit the values to the computer, and the next instruction in sequence will be executed. The Enter key is sometimes marked ↵ or may be called Return, as on a typewriter.

In summary, the second line (line 20 in BASICA) displays a message to the user on the screen, and the third line (line 30 in BASICA) accepts input. Figure 3.2 is an example of what might be entered and how it would be stored in the computer when the PRINT and INPUT instructions are executed.

The next five instructions in the sample program are treated as a unit:

```
Line numbers     {   40       WHILE HOURS < 999
for BASICA           .          .
                     .          .
                     .          .
                     80       WEND
```

The WHILE . . . WEND loop in QBASIC and BASICA is called a **logical control construct**. It instructs the computer to execute the series of steps between the WHILE instruction on the fourth line (line 40 of the BASICA program) and the WEND instruction on the eighth line (line 80 of the BASICA program) and to continue executing these instructions for as long as the specified condition on the WHILE line is met. The WHILE in the example tests to see if the HOURS entered is less than 999 (< is the symbol for less than). This means that the instructions within the WHILE . . . WEND will be executed repeatedly until HOURS is entered

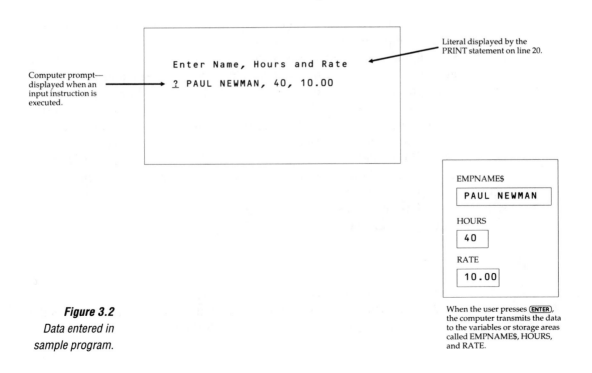

Computer prompt—
displayed when an
input instruction is
executed.

Enter Name, Hours and Rate

? PAUL NEWMAN, 40, 10.00

Literal displayed by the
PRINT statement on line 20.

EMPNAME$

PAUL NEWMAN

HOURS

40

RATE

10.00

When the user presses (ENTER),
the computer transmits the data
to the variables or storage areas
called EMPNAME$, HOURS,
and RATE.

Figure 3.2
*Data entered in
sample program.*

as 999 or more—999 or more entered in HOURS is the way we tell the computer we have no more input. In other words, each time that a value less that 999 is entered for HOURS, the instructions between the WHILE and the WEND will be executed. We use a value of 999 or higher in HOURS to terminate processing of the WHILE . . . WEND loop.

Let us review the way the sample program works. The program begins with a comment that describes the processing to be performed. It then displays a message to the user, who should then input a set of values for the first employee. The WHILE . . . WEND processes this first set of data, prints the result, and then transmits the next employee's data that the user inputs. This WHILE . . . WEND structure is executed repeatedly until the three values that are entered include a quantity of 999 or more for the number of hours worked. The value of 999 is intended to signal the computer that there is no more input to process.

Instructions within the WHILE . . . WEND are indented just to highlight the fact that they are under the control of a logical control structure. Programs written in QBASIC and BASICA are not, however, affected by indentation or spacing.

The value 999 in the HOURS variable is called a **trailer** or **sentinel value**. The user should enter it only after all valid data values have been read and processed. A value of 999 for HOURS indicates that there is no more data. The number 999 was selected as a trailer or sentinel value because it could never be an actual value. It signals an end-of-job condition since it is impossible for any employee to actually work 999 or more hours in any given week. A value of −999 or 8888 or any other *invalid* number of hours could have been chosen instead to signal an end-of-job condition.

Thus the instructions within the WHILE . . . WEND will be executed repeatedly until the user enters a trailer or end-of-job value of 999 for the HOURS variable. Suppose we use this program to process 15 employee entries. To end the run we might enter STOP,999,999 as the last line; that is, the 15 employee lines would be followed by a 16th trailer line entered as STOP,999,999. This would cause the WHILE . . . WEND to terminate because HOURS would be equal to 999. Note that all three entries—EMPNAME$, HOURS, RATE—must be entered when the INPUT instruction is executed, even though only HOURS is tested for an end-of-job value by the WHILE. It is the value of 999 in the variable called HOURS that terminates the loop.

The main body of all of our programs will follow this same structured format:

```
         INPUT (first set of values)
        ⎧ WHILE (one variable is not equal to a trailer value)
        ⎪    (process data)
 loop  ⎨    INPUT (next set of values)
        ⎩ WEND
         .
         .
         .
```

The pseudocode planning tool for most of our programs will also have the same form. WHILE . . . WEND will be used to denote a loop in a pseudocode structure.

All other words used in pseudocode (such as input, enter, and read) need not follow any specific rules:

• **Pseudocode**

```
Enter input
WHILE there is still input

   .
   .
   .

   Enter input
WEND
```

The first instruction within the WHILE . . . WEND of our QBASIC or BASICA programs processes the first set of data variables:

```
LET WAGES = HOURS * RATE
```

The fifth line in the program (line 50 in the BASICA program) calculates WAGES as the HOURS worked times the hourly RATE. The * is the symbol for multiplication. The LET or assignment statement will be discussed in detail later.

Let us walk through the logic in the program to see how the data is processed. When the INPUT instruction is executed, the computer prompts the user for input and the user keys in the values for the three variables, as illustrated previously.

Program Instruction	**Example of User-supplied Input**
INPUT EMPNAME$, HOURS, RATE	? JAY LENO, 40, 8.00

The LET instruction on the fifth line (line 50 in the BASICA program) calculates WAGES as 40 × 8.00, which is 320. The computer stores the result in the variable called WAGES.

The sixth line (line 60 in the BASICA program) is an output operation that prints on the printer a combination of literals or string constants and the contents of the variables called EMPNAME$ and WAGES:

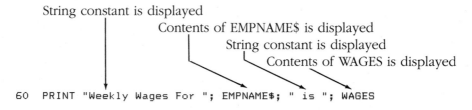

Each PRINT displays one line on a screen. While a PRINT displays data on a screen, an LPRINT prints data on a printer. We could, therefore, use an LPRINT to direct output to a printer rather than to the screen.

Constants (fixed data) or messages to be printed or displayed are enclosed in quotation marks. Hence, LPRINT "Weekly Wages For " will print the words enclosed in quotes. LPRINT EMPNAME$ will print the contents of the variable called EMPNAME$. Elements to be printed or displayed are most often separated by semicolons.

The above instruction will display the following:

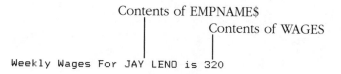

```
Weekly Wages For JAY LENO is 320
```

The seventh line (line 70 in the BASICA program) inputs the next set of values for Employee Name, Hours Worked, and Hourly Rate:

```
INPUT EMPNAME$, HOURS, RATE
```

Recall that the user enters the values for EMPNAME$, HOURS, and RATE all on one line, separated by commas. The three values will be transmitted to the computer when the Enter key is pressed.

The eighth line (line 80 in the BASICA program) indicates the end of the WHILE structure or loop:

```
WEND
```

When the program encounters the WEND statement or loop terminator, it repeats the series of instructions beginning with WHILE if the specified condition (HOURS < 999 in this case) is still met. That is, the next set of input is entered when the instruction on line 70 is executed, and the instructions within the WHILE loop are repeated if the HOURS entered on line 70 is less than 999.

Hence, when the computer executes WEND, control returns to the WHILE statement, which processes the next set of input if the HOURS just entered is less than (<) 999. Suppose HOURS is entered for the second employee as a number less than 999. Then the second set of input will be processed and a second line will be printed. A third set of input values will then be read. The process of calculating and printing WAGES and reading new input is repeated until the user enters 999 or more for HOURS. At that point, the WHILE ... WEND is terminated and the statement following the WEND is executed. The statement following the WEND is another PRINT instruction:

```
PRINT "End of Report"
```

This will display the literal or constant "End of Report" as the last printed line after all weekly wages are printed. This PRINT instruction is executed only after the WHILE ... WEND is terminated; that is, when the user enters a value for HOURS that is 999 or more, along with an EMPNAME$ and RATE, the final PRINT is executed.

The last instruction in a BASIC program is an END instruction:

END

We include this instruction in all our programs to explicitly indicate when a program is complete.

4

A Review of the Elements of a BASIC Program

BASIC programs include the following elements:

- Line numbers. These are required for BASICA but are optional for QBASIC and most other versions. We recommend that you omit them unless you are using BASICA.

- Comments. These provide information about the program. Comments begin with an apostrophe or single quote mark, or with REM for REMARK. Comments can be on a line by themselves or at the end of any instruction line. To highlight comments, we sometimes use the * or = characters as borders:

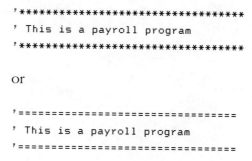

```
' *********************************
' This is a payroll program
' *********************************
```

or

```
' =================================
' This is a payroll program
' =================================
```

- Reserved words, also called key words. These have special meaning to the translator (compiler or interpreter) and are used to perform operations (e.g., PRINT, INPUT, WHILE, LET, LPRINT, WEND, END). As a convention, we use uppercase letters for reserved words. QBASIC and BASICA automatically convert letters in reserved words to uppercase letters.

- Variables. These are areas in storage to hold data (for example, EMPNAME$, HOURS, RATE, WAGES). As a convention, we use uppercase letters for variables, too. In addition, a $ must be used at the end of a variable that holds either alphabetic data or data that may contain letters, digits, and special characters; such data is called alphanumeric data.

- Operators. These may be used in arithmetic:

+   (addition)
−   (subtraction)
*   (multiplication)
/   (division)
^   (exponentiation)

- Constants. Data that is fixed in the program (for example, the trailer value of 999 on the fourth line of the sample program and the literal "End of Report" on the ninth line).

- Relational tests. These can be performed in a WHILE ... WEND loop and in conditional tests (such as WHILE HOURS < 999). Relational tests include

<   (less than)
<=   (less than or equal to)
>   (greater than)
>=   (greater than or equal to)
=   (equal to)
<>   (not equal to)

Every version of BASIC is free-form, which means that no spacing rules are required. We recommend, however, that you include spaces between elements of an instruction for ease of reading. 10LET A=B+7 is not as easy to read as 10 LET A = B + 7. Similarly, we recommend that you indent instructions within logical control constructs like WHILE ... WEND for ease of reading.

5

Interacting with Your Computer's Operating System and BASIC Translator

To run your BASIC programs you will be using an IBM microcomputer or compatible, another type of micro, or a larger mini or mainframe. Let us begin by focusing on how to use BASIC on IBM micros.

DOS Versions of BASIC for IBM Micros and Their Compatibles

Three DOS versions of BASIC can be used with IBM and IBM-compatible micros: BASIC and BASICA for DOS 4 and lower, and QBASIC for DOS 5 and higher.

BASIC, BASICA, and QBASIC

One version of BASIC is built into ROM (read-only memory) on IBM PCs and some IBM PS/2s, but not usually on their compatibles. This version is called simply BASIC (not BASICA). You can access this version by booting up a diskette-only system with no disks in any drive. The following message appears.

```
The IBM Personal Computer BASIC
Version A3.30 Copyright IBM Corp. 1981, 1982, 1983, 1984, 1985, 1986, 1987
60225 Bytes free


Ok
```

This version is very limited, and we do not recommend that you use it. For one thing, it does not enable you to save programs easily; thus, it is useful only as a learning tool. You can access this same limited version of BASIC from the DOS operating system (version 4 or lower) when using an IBM micro by typing BASIC at the A>, B>, or C> prompt, depending on where your operating system is located.

BASICA for IBM PCs or GW-BASIC for IBM-compatibles is also a BASIC translator supplied along with the DOS operating system (version 4 and lower). To access it, first load the operating system, then type BASICA (or GW-BASIC) in response to the A>, B>, or C> prompt, depending on where your operating system is located. The BASICA (or GW-BASIC) interpreter will then be loaded in as a program, and the screen display in Figure 5.1 will appear.

To run QBASIC for DOS 5 and higher, type QBASIC. Press Enter to display help screens or Esc (the Escape key) to go to the main menu.

Making Corrections to a Program

At this point you can begin to enter your program line by line. Each line is transmitted to the CPU when you press the Enter key.

Correcting an Error on the Current Line If you make a mistake before pressing the Enter key, you can use the Backspace key to erase characters up to the error, or you can use the cursor arrow keys (→ or ←) to return to an error point and fix the error. The cursor arrow keys do not erase characters as the cursor moves, but the Backspace key does erase. To replace one character with another, use the cursor arrow key to move to the character to be replaced and then key in the replacement. To add or delete characters, use the cursor arrow keys to go to the point of insertion or deletion; then press the Ins key and the character to be inserted, or the Del key to delete a character.

Correcting an Error on a Line Other Than the Current One If you realize an error has been made after you press the Enter key, follow these instructions:

- QBASIC: Use the cursor arrow keys (↑, ↓, →, ←) to return to the error point and simply fix the error.

- BASICA: Rekey the entire line with the same line number at any point in the program. If more than one line 30 appears in a program, for example, the last one *replaces* all previous references to that line. Be sure you press the Enter key

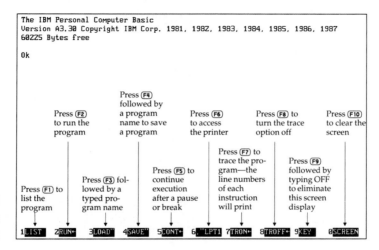

Figure 5.1
BASICA screen display.

at the end of the line after the change has been made; if you do not, the change or changes will not be transmitted.

Inserting an Instruction Line in a Program If you need to insert a line between two previously entered lines, follow these procedures:

- QBASIC: Go to the end of the first line and press Enter; a blank line will appear.

- BASICA: Give the new line an appropriate line number and key it in at any point. Say you need two additional instructions between line numbers 20 and 30. Enter them at any point as lines 24 and 28. Remember that in BASICA, instructions are executed in line number sequence regardless of the order in which they are entered.

Deleting an Instruction Line If you want to delete a line in QBASIC, go to the line and press Ctrl+Y (i.e., press the Ctrl key and while it is still depressed, press the letter Y). In BASICA, just reenter the line number with no instructions following the number.

System Commands

BASICA Instructions such as INPUT, PRINT, and so on are used to process data with all versions of BASIC. There are also BASIC **commands** for communicating with the specific translator itself. For example, to run a program in BASICA you must type a RUN command, which would not have a line number because it is not an instruction. Commands in BASIC do not have line numbers.

Several BASICA commands appear on the bottom of the screen; you can execute them by typing either the command or pressing a function key. Refer to Figure 5.1 which indicates how the function keys can be used for executing some commands.

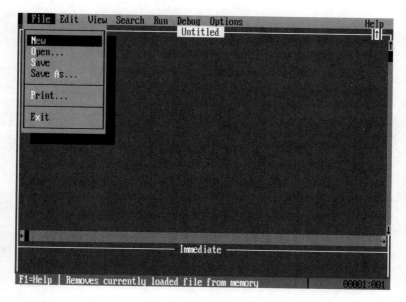

Figure 5.2
The QBASIC File command. Items may be selected from the pull-down menu.

Important BASICA system commands that you will need for running programs include the following:

- RUN—To execute a program (you may press the F2 function key in place of typing **RUN**).

- LIST—To display on the screen the program in line number sequence (you may press the F1 function key in place of typing **LIST**).

- LLIST—To print on a printer the program in line number sequence.

- NEW—To enter an entirely new program.

- SAVE "program name"—To save a BASICA program: a program name can be 1 through 8 characters long; preface the name with a drive letter if necessary (such as SAVE "B:PROG1"); the system automatically adds an extension of .BAS (you may press the F4 function key in place of typing **SAVE**).

- LOAD "program name"—To load back into memory a previously saved program (you may press the F3 function key in place of typing **LOAD**).

- SYSTEM—To leave BASICA and return to DOS.

QBASIC In QBASIC seven major commands appear on the top of the screen:

```
File      Edit      View      Search      Run      Debug      Options
```

To execute any of these, press the Alt key, and while it is depressed, press the first letter of the command. Alt+F executes the File command, Alt+V executes the View command, and so on. Once you are in command mode by pressing Alt+F, E, V, S, R, D, or O, you can use the → or ← cursor arrows to go to a different

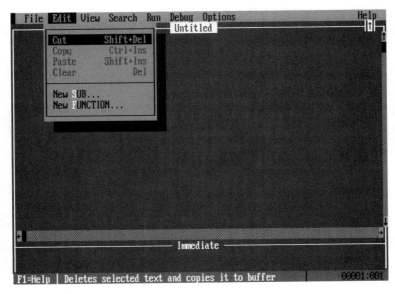

Figure 5.3
The QBASIC Edit command pull-down menu.

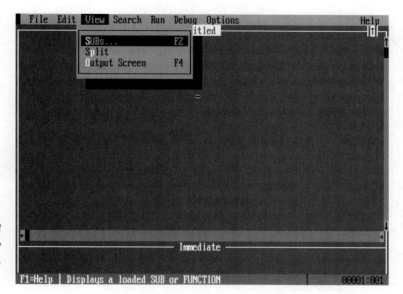

Figure 5.4
The QBASIC View command pull-down menu.

command. When a command is highlighted, pull-down menus or subcommands will appear and can be selected by highlighting them with the ↓ or ↑ cursor arrows and pressing Enter. See Figures 5.2 through 5.8, which illustrate the pull-down menus for each QBASIC command. The menu format for QBASIC is similar to the one for QuickBASIC and is discussed in detail at the end of this book.

With pull-down menus, pressing the highlighted letter of a particular subcommand or entry selects it. This selection method can be used in place of highlighting the entry and pressing the Enter key. Pull-down menu items shown in light gray (in Figures 5.2 through 5.8) are not available from the point at which you are cur-

Figure 5.5
The QBASIC Search command pull-down menu.

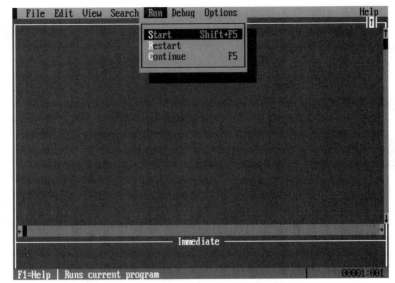

Figure 5.6
*The QBASIC Run
command pull-
down menu.*

rently located. That is, only highlighted items can be selected; items in light gray are not currently available. See Appendix B.

Pressing F1 at any point will give you context-sensitive help, which is information pertaining to the specific command you are executing when you request help.

Entering and Running a BASIC Program Using Another Translator or Computer

If you are using a version of BASIC other than QBASIC or BASICA, or a different type of computer, you will probably find that many BASIC commands are either identical (such as RUN) or very similar.

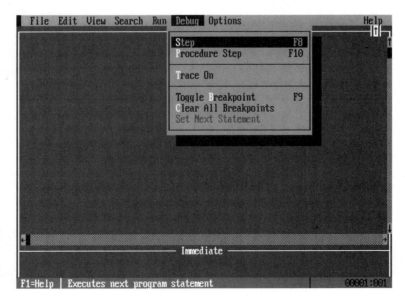

Figure 5.7
*The QBASIC
Debug command
pull-down menu.*

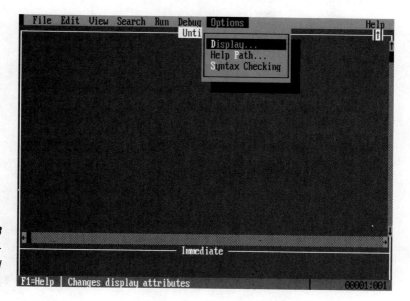

Figure 5.8
The QBASIC Options command pull-down menu.

The following is a brief list of questions to ask before beginning a BASIC session:

1. How to log on (for mainframes or networks) or boot up (for micros).

2. How to access or load in the BASIC translator.

3. How to transmit a line (usually by pressing the Enter key).

4. How to make insertions and deletions to a program file.

5. How to perform full-screen text editing (typically you use cursor arrow keys to move to the error point and then either replace, insert, or delete characters as described previously).

6. How to save a program and load it back into memory. With BASICA, press the F4 function key and name the program with an eight-character name. With QBASIC, press Alt+F for File then S for Save, and name the program with an eight-character name. To load a program back into memory with BASICA, press the F3 function key and the program name. With QBASIC, press Alt+F then O (for Open the file name).

7. How to run a program using test data. Press the F2 function key with BASICA or type RUN. With QBASIC, press Alt+R then the Enter key, or press the Shift+F5 keys to run the program.

6

A Brief Overview of Pseudocode as a Program Planning Tool

Regardless of the language in which they are written, programs should be planned before they are written, using a planning tool like pseudocode to map out the logic. Pseudocode, as a planning tool, is particularly useful in helping programmers determine the best type of structure for their programs. Moreover, for complex programs, pseudocode is essential for ensuring that the program is properly designed.

Several fundamental rules will guide you in reading and writing pseudocode:

- Pseudocode begins with a START and ends with a STOP.

- All instructions within the pseudocode are read in sequence.

- There is no set rule for specifying instructions in pseudocode. For example, "Enter input," "Read data," and "Input a name" are all acceptable ways for specifying that an input instruction should be coded.

- In pseudocode, to indicate a loop or the repeated occurrence of a series of instructions for all valid input, we will write:

  WHILE there is still input

  .

  .

  .

  WEND

We selected WHILE and WEND as pseudocode expressions for a loop. "WHILE there is still input" could be written as "WHILE more data," or "WHILE not end-of-job," or any other phrase that conveys the same meaning.

- The instructions between the WHILE . . . WEND in the pseudocode are executed repeatedly until there is no more input to process. We indent these instructions in pseudocode, as in a program, so that the overall structure is highlighted.

27

- A conditional or test may be specified in pseudocode as:

```
IF   condition THEN
   .        ← Statements to be executed if the
   .                    condition is met
   .
ELSE
   .
   .        ← Statements to be executed if the
   .                    condition is not met
ENDIF
```

(More on this later.)

Consider these two examples of pseudocode.

Example 1

This example is the pseudocode for a program to calculate an average grade:

```
START
Enter three Exams
WHILE there is still more data
      Compute Average
      Print Average
      Enter three Exams
WEND
STOP
```

Example 2

This example is the pseudocode for a program that will calculate sales commission:

```
START
Enter a SalesAmount
WHILE there is still more data
      IF   SalesAmount > 100.00 THEN
          Commission = .10 × SalesAmount
      ELSE
          Commission = .05 × SalesAmount
      ENDIF
      PRINT Commission
      Enter a SalesAmount
WEND
PRINT "End of Job"
STOP
```

Self-test

1. (T or F) Structured programs are sometimes called GOTO-less programs.
2. Some versions of BASIC are translated using a(n) _____, which scans the code and executes it all in one process; more efficient versions are translated by using a _____, which translates first, then executes the program, and can also save the program in executable form.
3. (T or F) QBASIC and BASICA instructions are compatible with most popular interpreted versions of BASIC for IBM microcomputers.
4. The two most common tools for planning a program are _____ and _____.
5. BASIC is an acronym for _____.
6. (T or F) Structured programs are easier to read, debug, modify, and maintain than nonstructured programs.
7. (T or F) Line numbers are required in BASICA but optional with QBASIC.
8. The _____ instruction is used to display information on the screen, while the _____ instruction writes the information on the printer.
9. A comment in BASIC begins with _____ or _____.
10. In the instruction WHILE AMT < 9999, 9999 is called a _____. The WHILE . . . WEND loop will be executed repeatedly until _____.

Solutions

1. T
2. interpreter; compiler
3. T
4. pseudocode; hierarchy charts
5. Beginner's All-Purpose Symbolic Instruction Code
6. T
7. T
8. PRINT; LPRINT
9. REM or ' (apostrophe)
10. trailer or sentinel value; the user enters an AMT as 9999 or more

Hands-on Assignment

Key in on your computer the sample payroll program discussed in this text, run it with sample data, save it, and reload it back into memory.

7

Writing Elementary BASIC Programs

In the following sections you will gain experience in BASIC by writing simple programs. First we will look at a few general programming principles.

Input-Process-Output

Most programs read in data, or **input**, process it in some way, and produce information called **output**. Input can be entered as a series of entries using a keyboard, as shown in Figure 7.1. Input can also be read in from a disk file or other storage medium, as shown in Figure 7.2.

Input is processed by either performing arithmetic operations or selecting operations to be performed, depending on the contents of the input. In the sample payroll program that was illustrated previously, an input variable called HOURS was multiplied by an input variable called RATE to produce an output field called WAGES. Output can be information that is displayed on a screen, printed on a printer, or stored on disk or other storage medium for future processing.

In this section we consider some elementary input, processing, and output operations. After you have read the section, you will be able to write simple BASIC programs in their entirety.

All of our programs use the structured programming technique discussed in the previous chapters:

```
INPUT . . .            'This is the initial read
WHILE there is still input
        process input
        produce output
        INPUT . . .
WEND
```

Defining Variable Names

The concept of a variable is very important in BASIC. The following sections discuss how to define variable names as well as what types of variables are allowed.

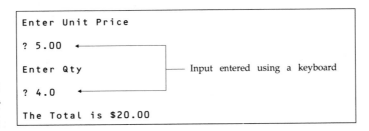

Figure 7.1
Entering input from a keyboard.

File of Accounts Receivable Records on Disk							
Record 1				Record 2			
ACCTNO	NAME	UNIT PRICE	QTY	ACCTNO	NAME	UNIT PRICE	QTY
001	NEWMAN, PAUL	3.00	2	002	EVANS, LINDA	5.50	2

Figure 7.2
Entering input from records on disk.

Overview of Variables

A variable is a data element that may be different each time the program is run. For example, customer numbers, prices of items, quantities, and so on may be read in as variable input each time the program is run. Similarly, the output information is variable because it depends on the input.

Variable data elements are given variable names in a program. If you say INPUT PRICE, for example, PRICE is called a variable name. Each variable name refers to a location or address in the computer's memory where the data is actually stored. Data elements or variables can be read in as input, given a value as a result of some processing, or produced as output.

The rules for defining variable names depend on whether the data to be stored is numeric or alphanumeric. A **numeric variable** contains numbers, an optional decimal point, and an optional plus or minus sign; such variables may be used in arithmetic operations. An **alphanumeric variable,** or **string variable,** can contain letters or symbols as well as numbers and is never used in arithmetic operations. A variable that contains an address or a name, for example, is considered alphanumeric.

Numeric Variables

We begin by considering the rules for forming numeric variable names, which are areas in storage that store numeric values.

- The name must begin with a letter.

- In QBASIC and BASICA the name can contain up to 39 characters; other versions of BASIC may have different length limitations.

- The name can use periods as word separators (such as SALES.AMT).

- Blanks are not permitted within a variable name (for example, the variable NEWSALARY is okay, as is NEW.SALARY, but NEW SALARY is not).

- BASIC's reserved words, such as INPUT or PRINT, are not permitted as variable names. In Appendix A, we list all QBASIC and BASICA reserved words.

Try to use meaningful names to define variables. They will make your programs easier to read and debug.

Recall that all versions of BASIC are case-insensitive. That means that you can use uppercase and lowercase letters interchangeably. Uppercase and lowercase letters are recognized by the BASIC translator as the same characters. To the translator, then, the variable Amt is the same as AMT or even AMt. The BASICA interpreter, however, converts all variables as well as reserved words to uppercase.

The following are examples of invalid numeric variable names:

Invalid Name	Reason
UNIT.PRICE.IN.$	The $ is not permitted in a numeric variable name. (UNIT.PRICE.IN.DOLLARS is okay.)
2NDAMT	A numeric variable must begin with a letter. (AMT2 is okay.)
EMPLOYEE WAGES	Blanks are not permitted within a numeric variable name. (EMPLOYEE.WAGES or EMPLOYEEWAGES is okay.)
OUTPUT	This is a BASIC reserved word. (OUTPUTAMT or OUTPUT.AMT is okay.)

String Variables

The variables discussed in the preceding section are used to store numeric data. These numeric variables can be used in arithmetic operations. Other variables, however, are needed to store alphanumeric data (letters, blanks, and/or special symbols, as well as numbers). These are called **string variables**.

String variable names are formed according to the same rules as those for numeric variables except that a string variable name ends with a $. Thus, EMPLOY-EENAME$, ADDRESS$, and MARITAL.STATUS$ are all valid names for string variables.

Defining Literals or String Constants

As you have seen, a literal or string constant is a value that is always the same regardless of the input. It is coded directly in the program as a fixed value. The value 999 that was used in the instruction WHILE HOURS < 999 is an example of a numeric constant. Similarly, the value "End of Report" in the PRINT "End of Report" instruction is an example of a string constant.

Just as there are two types of variables (numeric and string) in a BASIC program, there are two types of constants:

Type of Constant	Valid Characters	Examples
Numeric constant	Digits	46
	An optional decimal point	12.47
	An optional + or − sign to the *left* of the number	−12.3
String constant	Any set of characters enclosed in double quotes (")—digits, blanks, and special symbols, such as %, #, and @	"This is a Constant" "Input Error #412"

The Input Statement

An INPUT statement is used first to prompt the user for input and then to enter data to be processed. Both numeric variables and string variables can be entered as input, as in the following examples:

```
INPUT AMOUNT      'AMOUNT is a numeric variable
INPUT NAMEIN$     'NAMEIN$ is a string variable
```

When an INPUT statement is executed, the computer prompts the user for an entry. The prompt for input is displayed as a question mark (?) when the program is run. After the input is entered, the user must press the Enter key to transmit or send the data to the computer so that the next instruction in the program can be executed.

Entering Numeric Variables

The characters permitted in a numeric variable entered as input are the same as those for numeric constants:

Digits

An optional decimal point

An optional + or − sign to the left of the number

Hence, the following are all valid as numeric input that the user may key in as a response to a ? prompt:

$$115 \quad .25 \quad +1278 \quad 12.5 \quad -16.5$$

Each of these could be correctly entered into a numeric variable, such as AMOUNT.

Other characters, such as a comma or dollar sign, are not permitted in a numeric variable. Note again, characters that are valid as numeric input are also valid in a numeric constant. This means that the program itself could include numeric constants of 115, .25, and so on.

Let us consider the statement INPUT AMOUNT. Suppose you are prompted to enter a value for the AMOUNT variable during program execution, and you respond with any one of the following. The values will be *incorrect* for the reasons specified.

Incorrect Data Entry	Explanation
? 1,000	Commas are not permitted in numeric variables or numeric constants. The computer interprets the comma to mean the end of the value.
? a	a is not valid in a numeric field. Any nonnumeric input entered for a numeric variable is stored as 0.
? $12	The $ is not valid in a numeric field.
? 12−	The − is simply ignored because it is not to the left of the digits.

In each of these instances, the translator will respond

```
Redo from start
```

(or with some similar message) because an incorrect input value was entered.

When entering input, you can erase incorrect keystrokes with the Backspace key if you have not yet pressed the Enter key. It is best, then, to carefully check the input on the screen before pressing the Enter key.

Entering String Variables

A string or alphanumeric variable may also be entered as input. Recall that string variable names end with a $. When you input data to a string variable, any character is acceptable. The string variable that is stored may not be used in arithmetic operations, however, even if the value entered contains all numbers. The following, then, is not valid:

```
INPUT AMOUNT$
LET AMOUNTOUT = AMOUNT$ + 3   'AMOUNT$ may not be used in arithmetic
```

You will get a syntax error when the second instruction is translated by the computer because AMOUNT$, as a string variable, may not be used in an arithmetic operation.

You can also use quotation marks to delimit input strings. For example, consider the following:

```
INPUT CUST.NAME$
PRINT CUST.NAME$
```

Suppose you enter the following at the ? prompt.

```
? Newman, Paul
```

A *Redo from start* error message (or a similar error message) will be displayed because a comma was entered between the last and first names. Once the computer senses the comma, it assumes that the data to be entered in the variable CUST.NAME$ is complete. To enter string data that is itself to contain a comma, use quotation marks to delimit the value:

- **Program**

```
INPUT CUST.NAME$
PRINT CUST.NAME$
```

- **Run**

```
? "Newman, Paul"
Newman, Paul
```

The Assignment Statement

In BASIC, you can set a variable equal to a computed expression by using an assignment statement. This allows you to move data, copy it, and perform arithmetic operations, such as addition and subtraction, on it.

Performing BASIC Arithmetic Operations Using an Assignment Statement

The Format   Arithmetic operations are performed in BASIC by using a LET statement, which is also called an **assignment statement**. This type of instruction sets a variable equal to a computed value. The format of the instruction is as follows:

[LET] variable = expression

This statement is called a **format**. A format specifies the precise rules for using an instruction. The word LET, for example, is bracketed, which means that it is optional. The expression in the format consists of operators and operands (variables and constants) that compute a result.

The expression can operate on numeric variables and numeric constants with the following basic operators:

+	Addition
−	Subtraction
*	Multiplication
/	Division
^	Exponentiation

All variables and constants, including the resultant variable to the left of the equal sign, *must be numeric.* The caret (^) used for exponentiation is a special character above the number 6 on the main keyboard. Look at the following examples:

Valid Assignment Statements

LET TOTAL = AMT1 + AMT2

Explanation

The variable to the left of the equal sign, TOTAL, will be set equal to the sum of AMT1 and AMT2.

LET WAGES = HOURS * RATE +
    OVERTIME

An expression to the right of the equal sign can include more than one arithmetic operator. In this case, WAGES will be set equal to the computed result of HOURS × RATE + OVERTIME.

LET TAX = .05 * PRICE

An assignment statement can be used to set a variable equal to an expression that contains variables as well as constants. In this case, the variable PRICE is multiplied by the numeric constant .05, and the result is placed in TAX.

LET AREA = 3.14 * RADIUS ^ 2

This instruction computes the area of a circle as Pi × R^2 (Pi = 3.14 and R = the radius) and places the result in a numeric variable called AREA.

COMMISSION = SALES * .10

The word LET is optional in an assignment statement.

The following are *invalid* for the reasons noted:

Invalid Assignment Statements

LET .062 * SALARY = SOCSECTAX

Reason for Error

A variable, not an arithmetic expression, must appear after the word LET, that is, to the left of the equal sign. The correct statement is LET SOCSECTAX = .062 * SALARY.

LET NEWSALARY = $1,000 + SALARY

$1,000 is not a valid numeric constant because it includes a $ and a comma. The correct statement is LET NEWSALARY = 1000 + SALARY.

LET OVERTIME = 2HOURS

If 2HOURS means "2 times HOURS," the multiplication symbol, *, is necessary (such as in LET OVERTIME

= 2 * HOURS). Note also that 2HOURS cannot be a numeric variable because all variables must begin with a letter.

```
LET BONUS$ = AMT / 10
```

BONUS$ may not be the result of an arithmetic operation because it is a string or alphanumeric variable.

A Sample Program That Performs Arithmetic Operations Let us consider a program that reads in a series of Celsius temperatures and displays their Fahrenheit equivalents. End the program when a Celsius temperature of 999 is entered as a trailer or sentinel value. Recall that a trailer value indicates that there is no more data to process; it is entered after all "real" data has been input and processed. This value should not itself be processed as "real" data. The formula for calculating Fahrenheit temperature is:

$$Fahrenheit = (9/5 * Celsius) + 32$$

Recall that all our programs are structured. This means that we use an initial INPUT statement to read in the first Celsius value; we then use a WHILE . . . WEND loop to process this first value and to read additional values until there is no more input. We will use a basic PRINT statement in our examples to output the results on the screen. Other output options are discussed later. The pseudocode for this problem is as follows:

```
START
      Input a Celsius value
      WHILE there is more input
            Calculate Fahrenheit
            Print the result
            Input a Celsius value
      WEND
      Print a closing message
STOP
```

Standard pseudocode should begin with a START and end with a STOP. The instructions within the WHILE . . . WEND are part of a logical control sequence called a loop. The words used in each instruction need not follow any programming language's syntax because pseudocode, as a planning tool, is language independent.

The QBASIC or BASICA program follows. (Remember that line numbers are optional with QBASIC—we recommend you omit them; BASICA requires line numbers.)

```
INPUT CELSIUS
WHILE CELSIUS < 999
```

```
      LET FAHRENHEIT = 9/5 * CELSIUS + 32
      PRINT FAHRENHEIT
      INPUT CELSIUS
WEND
PRINT "That's all folks!"
END
```

In this program, 999, 9, 5, and 32 are numeric constants, and CELSIUS and FAHRENHEIT are numeric variables. "That's all folks!" is a string constant. Because the fraction 9/5 could be written as 1.8, the third line could also be coded as LET FAHRENHEIT = 1.8 * CELSIUS + 32.

After the program has been translated and there are no syntax errors, it is ready to be run. When the computer executes the INPUT instruction, a ? prompt appears on the screen. This means that the computer is waiting for input from the user. The input expected on each line must be in numeric form with no special symbols included (no commas or dollar signs, for example).

Suppose you enter 25 at the cursor point or prompt. After you press the Enter key, 25 is transmitted to and stored in the variable named CELSIUS. Then the FAHRENHEIT equivalent of the CELSIUS temperature of 25 is computed.

The PRINT instruction will print the value 77 (9/5 × 25 + 32). The next INPUT instruction on the fifth line will cause the prompt to appear again, which is a request for another CELSIUS temperature. This series of instructions, or loop, continues repeatedly until you enter a CELSIUS temperature of 999 (or more); the trailer value of 999 terminates the loop and causes the closing string constant or message ("That's all folks!") to print.

Using indented instructions within the loop makes it easier to understand the program's structure. Indentation is most easily accomplished by pressing the key marked Tab on the left-hand side of the keyboard.

Self-test

Solutions to questions 1 and 2 require full BASIC programs. In each case, the program should be able to process numerous input variables. All programs should be structured. Begin by planning the program with pseudocode. Use a WHILE ... WEND loop to enable the program to continue processing other values that need to be entered as input.

1. Write a program to input the number of gallons of gas used in a trip and the number of miles traveled. Print miles per gallon.
2. Write a program to input sales amounts and to print a commission as 15 percent of each sales amount.

Solutions

1. Pseudocode:

> START
> Enter No of Gallons and Miles Traveled

```
                              WHILE there is still input
                                      Calculate Miles Per Gallon
                                      Print the result
                                      Enter No of Gallons and Miles Traveled
                              WEND
                              Print an end-of-run message
                      STOP
```

QBASIC Program (include line numbers with BASICA):

```
'  This program computes miles per gallon
INPUT NOOFGALLONS, MILESTRAVELED
WHILE NOOFGALLONS < 99
    MILESPERGALLON = MILESTRAVELED / NOOFGALLONS
    PRINT MILESPERGALLON
    INPUT NOOFGALLONS, MILESTRAVELED
WEND
PRINT "End of Job"
END
```

2. Pseudocode:

```
                      START
                              Enter Sales Amount
                              WHILE there is still input
                                      Calculate Commission
                                      Print the result
                                      Enter Sales Amount
                              WEND
                              Print an end-of-run message
                      STOP
```

QBASIC Program (include line numbers with BASICA):

```
' This program calculates Sales commissions
INPUT SALESAMOUNT
WHILE SALESAMOUNT < 99999
    COMMISSION = .15 * SALESAMOUNT
    PRINT COMMISSION
    INPUT SALESAMOUNT
WEND
PRINT "DONE!"
END
```

Hierarchy of Arithmetic Operations The sequence in which arithmetic operations are performed may affect the results of a computation. Consider the following:

```
INPUT AMT1, AMT2, AMT3
WHILE AMT2 <> 99
    LET TOTAL = AMT1 - AMT2 * AMT3
    PRINT TOTAL
    INPUT AMT1, AMT2, AMT3
WEND
END
```

Suppose we initially enter AMT1 as 10, AMT2 as 5, and AMT3 as 2. You need to determine whether the computer will perform AMT1 $-$ AMT2 * AMT3, which is equal to $10 - 5 \times 2$, as

$$(a)\ (10 - 5) \times 2 = 10$$

or

$$(b)\ 10 - (5 \times 2) = 0$$

If the computer performs the subtraction operation first as in (a) and then the multiplication, the result will be different from that obtained by performing the multiplication first as in (b).

Computers follow these hierarchy rules in most programming languages:

- Arithmetic operations are performed in the following order:

    1. Exponentiation first.
    2. Multiplication and division next.
    3. Addition and subtraction last.

- If an instruction has two or more operations on the same level, the operations are executed in sequence from left to right.

- The use of parentheses overrides all other hierarchy rules.

Let us look again at our previous assignment statement:

```
LET TOTAL = AMT1 - AMT2 * AMT3
```

According to the hierarchy rules, the multiplication is performed first and then the subtraction. That is, TOTAL will contain the following result when the arithmetic operations are executed:

$$10 - 5 * 2 = 10 - 10 = 0$$

As noted, the basic hierarchy rules can be overridden with the use of parentheses. Thus, to obtain AMT1 $-$ AMT2 multiplied by AMT3, we would write LET TOTAL = (AMT1 $-$ AMT2) * AMT3.

Example

Input three exam grades for every student in a class and calculate the average grade for each student. The pseudocode and BASIC program follow:

- **Pseudocode**

```
            START
                    Enter three Exam Grades
                    WHILE there is still data
                            Calculate Average
                            PRINT Average
                            Enter three Exam Grades
                    WEND
            STOP
```

- **QBASIC Program** (include line numbers with BASICA):

```
INPUT EXAM1, EXAM2, EXAM3          ' Get initial data
WHILE EXAM1 <> 999                 ' Check for trailer value
    LET AVERAGE = (EXAM1 + EXAM2 + EXAM3) / 3
    PRINT AVERAGE
    INPUT EXAM1, EXAM2, EXAM3
WEND
END
```

In this instance, the parentheses in the LET or assignment statement are required to obtain the proper order of evaluation. The following will *not* produce a correct average:

```
LET AVERAGE = EXAM1 + EXAM2 + EXAM3 / 3
```

Based on the hierarchy rules, the computer performs the additions before the division; hence, only EXAM3 would be divided by 3 if parentheses were omitted. Thus AVERAGE would be set equal to EXAM1 + EXAM2 + EXAM3 / 3—only EXAM3 is divided by 3.

In summary, when an operation or a series of operations is to be performed in an order different from those specified in the hierarchy rules, you enclose the operation(s) in parentheses. In the previous example, you want the three exams added before the division is performed, so you must use parentheses.

Note, too, that any attempt to divide by zero will result in an error.

Self-test

Indicate the result in questions 1 and 2.
1. 10 LET TOTAL1 = 4 + 2 / (5 − 3)
2. 10 LET TOTAL3 = 4 * 5 + 2

Indicate the error in questions 3 and 4.

3. 10 LET C = 2A + D

4. 10 PRINT "THE ANSWER IS ; F

Write a BASIC instruction to perform the following:

5. $A = \dfrac{3 + C}{D + 7}$

Solutions

1. 4 + 2 / 2 = 4 + 1 = 5
2. 4 * 5 + 2 = 20 + 2 = 22
3. 2A must be coded as 2 * A: 10   LET C = 2 * A + D
4. A quotation mark is missing: 10   PRINT "THE ANSWER IS "; F
5. 10 LET A = (3 + C) / (D + 7)   ' The parentheses are required

Incrementing Counters and Obtaining Running Totals As you have learned, an assignment statement can be used to perform an arithmetic operation and to place the result in the variable indicated. For example, the statement LET NET = PRICE − DISCOUNT causes DISCOUNT to be subtracted from PRICE and the result placed in NET.

You could also use an assignment or LET statement to replace the value in a variable. LET AMT = 30 places the value of 30 in AMT. Similarly, LET TOTAL1 = TOTAL2 copies the value stored in TOTAL2 into the variable called TOTAL1.

You could also use an assignment statement to place a string value into a string variable. LET CODE$ = "ABC" or LET CODE1$ = CODE2$ are valid statements.

Assignment statements can be used for incrementing the contents of a variable. Consider the following: LET COUNTER = COUNTER + 1. This statement is not a valid mathematical expression, but it is a valid BASIC statement that performs the following:

1. One is added to the value in the variable called COUNTER.

2. The sum of one plus the value in the variable COUNTER then replaces the original contents of COUNTER.

If COUNTER had an initial value of 10, 1 would be added to it and 11 would be placed back into COUNTER. In other words, the effect of the instruction LET COUNTER = COUNTER + 1 is to add one to COUNTER. This type of assignment statement is frequently used to increment counters or to add to totals. Similarly, the instruction LET TOTAL = TOTAL + AMT1 adds AMT1 to TOTAL.

In general, an assignment statement of this kind is used to obtain a running total that increments a variable, or adds to the contents of that variable. To accumulate the sum of all transaction amounts read in, for example, write:

```
LET SUM = 0           'Initialize SUM at 0
INPUT AMOUNT          'Get an initial AMOUNT
```

```
WHILE AMOUNT <> 999         'Trailer value for AMOUNT is 999
    LET SUM = SUM + AMOUNT   'Add AMOUNT to running total
    INPUT AMOUNT            'Get another input AMOUNT
WEND
PRINT SUM                   'Only one final total is printed
END
```

(Line numbers are required for BASICA.)

Each time the computer executes the WHILE . . . WEND loop, SUM is increased by the value of each AMOUNT that is entered as input. Thus, the LET instruction on the fourth line accumulates a running total of all values of AMOUNT the user enters.

The first program line is used to initialize the variable called SUM at 0. Although BASIC automatically initializes numeric variables at 0, it is always good practice to explicitly set to 0 all variables that will be used as running totals. Other programming languages may not initialize variables automatically, so we advise programmers to develop the habit of setting numeric variables to 0 before adding to them. Note, however, that a variable such as AMOUNT in this program need not be initialized because it will always contain values the user enters.

Example

For all salaries that are entered, provide for a $100 raise and print the new salaries. The pseudocode and BASIC program are shown next.

- **Pseudocode**

```
START
    Enter Salary
    WHILE there is still input
        Increase Salary by $100
        Print New Salary
        Enter Salary
    WEND
STOP
```

- **QBASIC Program** (use line numbers for BASICA)

```
'This program increases each salary by $100
INPUT SALARY                    'Get initial Salary data
WHILE SALARY < 999999           'Test for trailer value
    NEWSALARY = SALARY + 100
    PRINT NEWSALARY
    INPUT SALARY                'Get more data
WEND
END
```

CODING GUIDELINES FOR ASSIGNMENT STATEMENTS

- The word LET is optional in an assignment statement. It is best to either use it consistently or omit it in all your programs.

- Spaces are not required on either side of the arithmetic operators (=, *, +, and so on), but they will make your program easier to read if you use them (for example, AMT = 5 * PRICE rather than AMT=5*PRICE).

Self-test

For both questions, full programs are required. In each case, the program should be able to process numerous input variables. All programs should be structured. Begin by planning the program with pseudocode.

1. Write a program to input numerous lines of data where each line contains an employee's name, gross pay, and taxes. Print, on the printer, each employee's name and net pay, where net pay = gross pay − taxes.
2. Input Daily Sales totals for Monday, Tuesday, Wednesday, Thursday, and Friday all on a single line. Display the Average Daily Sales on the screen.

Solutions

1. Pseudocode:

```
START
        Enter Name, GrossPay and Taxes
        WHILE there is still input
                Calculate Net Pay
                Print the result
                Enter Name, Gross Pay and Taxes
        WEND
STOP
```

QBASIC Program (use line numbers for BASICA):

```
'This program calculates NetPay
INPUT EMPNAME$, GROSSPAY, TAXES
WHILE TAXES < 99999
    NETPAY = GROSSPAY - TAXES
    LPRINT EMPNAME$; NETPAY
    INPUT EMPNAME$, GROSSPAY, TAXES
WEND
END
```

2. Pseudocode:

> START
>> Enter 5 daily sales figures
>> WHILE there is still input
>>> Calculate an average
>>> Display the result
>>> Enter 5 daily sales figures
>> WEND
> STOP

QBASIC Program (use line numbers for BASICA):

```
'This program calculates average weekly sales
INPUT MSALES, TSALES, WSALES, THSALES, FSALES
WHILE MSALES < 99999
    AVERAGE = (MSALES + TSALES + WSALES + THSALES + FSALES) / 5
    PRINT AVERAGE
    INPUT MSALES, TSALES, WSALES, THSALES, FSALES
WEND
END
```

The PRINT and LPRINT Statements

The two fundamental ways to obtain output with BASIC are through PRINT, which displays output on a screen, and LPRINT, which prints output on a printer.

PRINT

All output generated by the PRINT instruction will appear on the screen. This output will be displayed interactively with any input that the user enters.

LPRINT

If the output is to be retained in hard-copy or printed form, use an LPRINT instruction in place of PRINT. You will see later that it is often more meaningful to print the input as well as the output on the printer so that the user has a hard-copy record of what each result means.

Rules for using the PRINT and LPRINT are identical, so we consider them together.

The format of the PRINT and LPRINT is as follows:

$$\left\{ \begin{array}{l} \text{PRINT} \\ \text{LPRINT} \end{array} \right\} \qquad \text{[expression list] [;]}$$

Both the PRINT and LPRINT instructions have the same format; that is, either PRINT or LPRINT could be used in the format shown.

The expression list may be a series of variables and/or literals; for example, PRINT AMT1 displays the contents of AMT1 and LPRINT "DONE!!" prints the literal or constant DONE!! The expression list also can be an arithmetic expression; for example, PRINT AMT1 * 2 will print the product of AMT1 × 2.

Items within a PRINT or LPRINT expression list may be separated by a semicolon or comma. We use semicolons as separators in our illustrations because a semicolon ensures that each entry appears directly to the right of the previous entry on a single line. Commas as separators place each expression in a separate zone that is 14 characters long.

The bracket in the PRINT format means that an expression list is optional. The instruction PRINT or LPRINT with no other entry will display or print a blank line.

When semicolons are used as separators, string variables and constants print adjacent to one another unless blanks or spaces are included. Consider this example:

Syntax

```
PRINT "Name is "; LASTNAME$
```

Meaning

Displays the string constant "Name is " along with the contents of the string variable LASTNAME$, both on the same line. The space after "Name is " in the constant is required because without it the Last Name would collide or print adjacent to the s in "is" (for example, Name isJohnson).

As noted, string variables and literals require a space as a separator in the expression list. Positive or unsigned numeric variables and constants, however, always print with a space before the value so that a " " or blank as a separator is not necessary. So, +12 or 12 entered as input will print as 12 with a leading blank.

Negative numbers, however, do not automatically print with a space before the number: provision must be made for appropriate spaces. If a variable called AMT, for example, will contain a negative number, code PRINT "The negative number is "; AMT, rather than PRINT "The negative number is"; AMT, which has no space after the s in "is."

In summary, all numbers, both positive and negative, are always followed by a space, but only positive numbers are always preceded by a space.

CODING GUIDELINES

- The rules about spaces before and after positive and negative numbers may be confusing and are often forgotten. To avoid any potential collisions, always include a space between all variables and values to be printed.

- Although an arithmetic operation may be included in a PRINT or LPRINT statement, we recommend that you separate such instructions into two statements:

```
LET TOTAL = AMT1 + AMT2
PRINT "The Total is "; TOTAL
```

rather than:

```
PRINT "The Total is "; AMT1 + AMT2
```

The former is easier to read and debug.

Making Output More Readable

You can use several techniques to make your output more readable, as shown in the following sections.

Printing Literals with Variables for More Meaningful Output

We typically PRINT (or LPRINT) a string expression along with a computed result to make the output more meaningful. For example, code PRINT "The Sum Is "; SUM, rather than PRINT SUM.

Printing Explanatory Messages to the User Before Data Is Entered as Input

We also use a PRINT instruction to provide the user with some information about how data is to be entered. Explanatory messages should precede the first INPUT statement when they are intended as instructions to the user.

- **Program** (use line numbers with BASICA)

```
PRINT "Enter Two Amount Fields Separated By a Comma"
PRINT "Enter 999, 999 When Done"
INPUT AMT1, AMT2              'Get initial amounts
WHILE AMT1 < 999             'Check trailer value
    TOTAL = AMT1 + AMT2
    PRINT "The Total Is "; TOTAL
    INPUT AMT1, AMT2         'Get additional Amounts
WEND
PRINT "End Of Job"
END
```

- **Run**

  Press Alt+R for Run, then press Enter (or Shift+F5) with QBASIC; press the F2 function key with BASICA.

- **Result**

```
Enter Two Amount Fields Separated By a Comma
Enter 999, 999 When Done
? 10, 15
The Total Is 25
? 999,999
End Of Job
```

The two explanatory PRINT statements are executed only once, at the beginning of the run, but you may repeat them within the loop before the second INPUT statement if you wish. This will result in the message printing before each input prompt.

Editing Printed Data

A record on a disk file may, for example, have two amount fields with the following data: 450 and 38726.58. Although these fields are acceptable as is in disk files, the printed report should contain this information in edited form to make it more meaningful to the user. That is, $450.00 and $38,726.58 are clearer methods of presenting the data.

Editing is the process of making fields of data clearer, neater, and more useful. In this section, we focus on the types of editing that can be performed on both numeric and string variables. The following editing functions will be discussed:

- Suppression of leading zeros.

- Printing a specified number of digits to the right of the decimal point regardless of the number of decimal digits in the variable.

- Printing commas and dollar signs.

The editing functions described in this section may be performed only on numeric variables or fields.

Consider the following example:

- **QBASIC Program** (line numbers are required with BASICA):

```
INPUT AMT
WHILE AMT <> 9
    LPRINT AMT
    INPUT AMT
WEND
END
```

- **Run**

```
? 12.75
? 0
? 125000
```

The output would appear on the printed page as:

```
12.75
0
125000
```

The results would be more readable if they were printed, instead, as follows:

```
$       12.75
$        0.00
$125,000.00
```

In the latter case, notice that the numbers are aligned on the decimal point, a dollar sign precedes each value, and a comma has been inserted in the last number to make it easier to read.

To do this type of editing, we use an LPRINT USING or PRINT USING statement.

The LPRINT USING and PRINT USING statements

The LPRINT USING and PRINT USING statements allow you to format and edit your output.

Formatting

Two of the major purposes of the LPRINT USING and PRINT USING statements are to provide proper alignment of results and to edit the results. In this context, editing means making the results more readable and useful by adding edit characters, such as dollar signs and commas.

The format for the LPRINT USING and PRINT USING is:

$$\left\{ \begin{matrix} \text{LPRINT} \\ \text{PRINT} \end{matrix} \right\} \text{USING format string; expression list [;]}$$

The format string is a string constant or variable that describes the way the expression list is to be formatted. The expression list includes the numeric variables to be printed. If more than one variable or field is to be printed on the line, they may be separated by commas, spaces, or semicolons. We typically use semicolons.

The format string that describes the editing to be performed is enclosed in double quotation marks (") and is followed by a semicolon, which is then followed by the variable(s) to be formatted.

As noted, the PRINT USING statement may use exactly the same format string as the LPRINT USING. The only difference is that with PRINT USING, the output is displayed rather than printed.

Formats the variable that follows it
Indicates the variable to be formatted

```
PRINT USING "######"; AMT
```

Editing Numeric Fields

Often you will need to edit numeric fields; for example, you might want to align numbers with each other. Editing is also performed to add commas and dollar signs.

Aligning the Contents of Numeric Variables The symbol # is used in the format string of the LPRINT USING or PRINT USING statement to indicate that a numeric variable is to be printed in right-justified or right-aligned form. Right-justified output is aligned so that the three numbers, 87, 387, and 2826, for example, would print as:

```
  87
 387
2826
```

Note that the numbers print with the rightmost, or units positions, aligned.

The symbol # in the format string not only right-justifies data but also replaces leading or leftmost zeros with blanks. Thus, 0026, 087, 382 would print as:

```
 26
 87
382
```

This type of editing ensures that all data is printed with units positions aligned properly and with leading zeros suppressed. The expression in the LPRINT USING or PRINT USING is separated from the variable by a semicolon. Consider the following:

```
LPRINT USING "######"; AMT
```

The values for AMT will print as follows:

Value of AMT	LPRINT or PRINT USING Format String	Printed Results
1234	"######"	1234
26	"######"	26
374	"######"	374
26873	"######"	26873
987261	"######"	987261
7522117	"######"	%7522117

Without PRINT USING, the output would print left-justified. The column marked "Value of AMT" has data listed in left-justified form, that is, with numbers aligned on the left. It is far more appropriate to print numbers right-justified so that the units position of each number prints in the same relative position, and the tens position of each number prints in the same relative position, and so forth. To get right-justification, use LPRINT USING or PRINT USING.

Note, again, that the rules for LPRINT USING and PRINT USING are the same. The format string "######" indicates that the value of the variable can be any number from one to six integers. If AMT has a value greater than six integers or whole numbers, such as 7522117 in the previous example above, it would print as %7522117. The % indicates that the variable is too large for the format string specified.

You can edit several variables with the same format string. For example, coding PRINT USING "######"; AMT1, AMT2, AMT3 will right-justify all three amount fields.

Aligning Fields with Decimal Places If the number to be printed contains a decimal point, include the decimal point in the format string along with the number of decimal positions to be printed, as in the following:

```
LPRINT USING "######.##"; AMT
```

Consider these examples:

Value of AMT	LPRINT or PRINT USING Format String	Printed Results
12.75	"######.##"	12.75
8.60	"######.##"	8.60
125000.50	"######.##"	125000.50
4	"######.##"	4.00
4.1	"######.##"	4.10
14.7685	"######.##"	14.77
87.67	"######.##"	87.67
−6.48	"######.##"	-6.48
−.25	"######.##"	-0.25

First, the format string right-justifies the number. Second, the results will print with exactly two decimal digits for each variable.

The variables in the expression list can each have up to six integers and any number of decimal places. That is, the number of integers in the variable should not exceed the number of #'s before the decimal point in the format string. In the examples, if the number of integers actually stored in the variable is more than six, then a % precedes the output to indicate that a size error has occurred. This means that the variable has too many integers for the formatted output string.

But the number of decimal positions (that is, positions to the right of the decimal point) in the variable itself is not limited. If there are more decimal digits in the variable than are specified in the format string, this is not considered an error. Suppose AMT has three or more decimal positions. A PRINT USING or LPRINT USING with ".##" means that the results will be rounded to two decimal places rather than truncated to two decimal places. Say AMT has a value of 12.755 and you code it as LPRINT USING "##.##"; AMT. Then, AMT will print as 12.76. If AMT has fewer than two decimal places, zeros will be added to print to two decimal places. An AMT equal to 4 will print as 4.00, and 4.1 will print as 4.10 using the above format string. If AMT has only decimal positions with no integers as in .25, it will print with a leading zero (0.25).

Double-Precision Numbers Single-precision numeric variables or fields are always accurate up to seven integers, but inaccuracies may occur if more integers are used. If you wish to store a numeric variable that has more than seven integers, you should establish the variable as a double-precision number. If a programmer does not define a long numeric variable as double precision, and the user enters a number with more than seven digits, it will print as what we call a floating-point number. In floating-point numbers, an E will denote where the decimal point should be positioned.

Consider this example:

```
INPUT AMT1
PRINT.AMT1
```

If AMT1 is entered as 111111111, which is a number larger than seven digits, it may print as 1.111111E+08. This means that the actual value can be obtained by moving the decimal point eight positions to the right. To avoid long numbers printing with the E (for exponential) format, define them as double precision by using a # at the end of the numeric variable name. AMT#, for example, is a double-precision numeric variable.

Follow this guideline: When there is a possibility that a variable may exceed seven whole numbers or integers, establish it as a double-precision variable.

Because of the way the computer represents numbers, you may find that large values, when edited, are rounded by the computer. Making the variables double precision avoids any rounding errors.

Inserting Commas in Numeric Fields If you want one or more commas to separate integers in a number that is displayed or printed, you can simply include the commas in the format string of the PRINT USING or LPRINT USING statement. All data will remain decimally aligned and right-justified.

Consider the following statement:

```
LPRINT USING "#,###.##"; AMT
```

If AMT has a value of 1500.50, for example, it will print as 1,500.50. Commas print only if the value of AMT has enough significant or nonzero integers; otherwise, commas are suppressed or replaced with blanks. Thus, if AMT has a value of 532.50, for example, it will print without the commas as ҍҍ532.50, where ҍ denotes a blank. All data will be aligned on the decimal point.

The following are examples of the LPRINT USING or PRINT USING where commas are to be printed:

Value of AMT	LPRINT or PRINT USING Format String	Printed Results
4872.83	"###,###.##;"	4,872.83
873586.487	"###,###.##;"	873,586.49
287.05	"###,###.##;"	287.05
31.621	"###,###.##;"	31.62
2876543.00	"###,###.##;"	%2,876,543.00

Note that % in the last example indicates that the variable is too long for the format string. The format string allows for a maximum of six integers or whole numbers (that is, six places to the left of the decimal point).

Inserting Dollar Signs in Numeric Fields   If you want a dollar sign to print with the contents of a field, include the dollar sign in the LPRINT or PRINT USING statement. For example,

```
LPRINT USING "$#,###.##"; AMT
```

If AMT contained a value of 3546.23, it would print as $3,546.23.

Consider the following examples:

Value of AMT	LPRINT or PRINT USING Format String	Printed Results
28.73	"$#,###.##"	$ 28.73
4872.26	"$#,###.##"	$4,872.26

Using a Floating Dollar Sign   Sometimes printing a dollar sign as we just did is not sufficient. If there is the possibility that blanks in the output can be tampered with, as on checks, for example, you would not want spaces between the $ and the first significant digit. If AMT contained 1.93, for example, the output would print as follows: $ 1.93. In this case, a series of blanks separates the dollar sign from the first significant character. Someone could easily type in values so that $ 1.93 would appear as $99991.93. This is particularly dangerous if the output is a check.

By including two dollar signs at the beginning of the format string of the LPRINT or PRINT USING statement, you can ensure that the dollar sign prints adjacent to the first significant character. In other words, the use of two dollar signs will cause the $ to float, suppressing both leading commas and leading zeros so that the $ prints next to the first significant digit of the number. In this instance, the $ is called a floating dollar sign.

Consider the following examples:

Value of AMT	LPRINT or PRINT USING Format String	Printed Results
28.73	"$$#,###.##"	$28.73
4872.26	"$$#,###.##"	$4,872.26
927.163	"$$#,###.##"	$927.16
.06	"$$#,###.##"	$0.06
87262.00	"$$#,###.##"	$87,262.00

To display or print two values on a single line, only one of which is to be edited, use two PRINT or LPRINT instructions where the first ends with a semicolon (;), which means that there is more to print on that line. For example,

```
PRINT NAME.IN$;
PRINT USING "##.##"; AMT
```

Both NAME.IN$ and AMT will be displayed on the *same line* because the first PRINT ends with a semicolon.

8

Selection Using the IF Statement

Some logical control structures allow you to write BASIC instructions that are executed conditionally. For example, if a certain condition is met, your program does one thing; if it is not met, your program does another. Such control structures give you a great deal of flexibility in writing programs that will perform different operations depending on specific conditions. In the next sections we examine these structures in detail.

Overview of the Four Logical Control Structures

Thus far you have learned syntax rules for a number of BASIC instructions. You have seen that instructions are executed in sequence unless a WHILE . . . WEND loop changes the order of execution. The order in which instructions can be executed is controlled by logical control structures. Four types of logical control structures may be used in any programming language:

- Sequence

- Selection (IF-THEN-ELSE)

- Iteration (WHILE . . . WEND or other loop)

- Case (ON GOSUB)

Sequence
The pseudocode specification for a sequence is as follows:

START
.
.   { Sequence of steps goes here
.
STOP

Consider the following example in QBASIC (use line numbers in BASICA):

```
'This program calculates a total
INPUT AMT1, AMT2
LET TOTAL = AMT1 + AMT2
PRINT "THE TOTAL IS "; TOTAL
END
```

All instructions are executed in **sequence** unless one of the other logical control structures such as the WHILE . . . WEND alters the order.

Selection
Selection is a logical control structure that executes instructions depending on whether a condition or conditions are met. Selection is sometimes referred to as an **IF-THEN-ELSE** structure because it has the following pseudocode format:

IF   (condition is met or is "true") THEN

.   { Indicates the sequence of instructions
.   to be executed only if the condition
.   is met or is "true"

ELSE

.   { Indicates the sequence of instructions to be executed
.   if the condition is not met or is "false"
.

ENDIF   Terminates the scope of the IF structure in a pseudocode

Most programming languages have an IF-THEN-ELSE logical control structure similar to this pseudocode. We discuss the selection structure in BASIC in this section, but first we will briefly outline the other two logical control structures so that you are aware of all four ways in which instructions can be executed.

Iteration
Iteration is the logical control structure that enables a sequence of instructions to be executed repeatedly. We have thus far used a WHILE . . . WEND loop for iteration. The next section will focus on the full range of BASIC instructions that can be used for iteration.

The pseudocode specification for a WHILE . . . WEND loop is:

WHILE condition is met

$$\cdot\ \left\{\text{Sequence of steps to be performed}\right.$$

WEND

An example in QBASIC or BASICA is (use line numbers in BASICA):

```
INPUT AMTIN
WHILE AMTIN < 99999
    PRINT AMTIN
    INPUT AMTIN
WEND
END
```

Case

A **case** structure is a logical control structure that enables the user to choose which task the computer should perform from a list of possible tasks. For example, suppose you are updating payroll data. The program may display a menu that indicates the type of update to be performed. Perhaps you will have to press 1 to change an employee's salary, press 2 to change an employee's name, and so on. The case structure is used to designate which path to follow, depending on a value entered by the user. We discuss this structure beginning on page 108.

The IF Statement

In this section we focus on the IF-THEN-ELSE (selection) structure, which permits you to execute an instruction or series of instructions depending on the contents of variables. The IF-THEN-ELSE structure is coded in BASIC with the IF statement.

The Instruction Format for an IF Statement

A **conditional statement** is one that performs operations depending on whether some condition is met or is "true." Such statements begin with the word IF and are called IF-THEN-ELSE, or selection, structures.

The basic instruction format for IF statements is as follows.

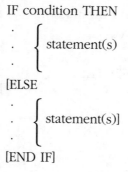

IF condition THEN

$$\cdot\ \left\{\text{statement(s)}\right.$$

[ELSE

$$\cdot\ \left\{\text{statement(s)}\right]$$

[END IF]

Several relational operators can be used in an IF expression.

Operand 1	Relational Operator	Operand 2	Meaning
literal-1 or variable-1	=	literal-2 or variable-2	IF Operand 1 equals Operand 2
	<		IF Operand 1 is less than Operand 2
	>		IF Operand 1 is greater than Operand 2
	<=		IF Operand 1 is less than or equal to Operand 2
	>=		IF Operand 1 is greater than or equal to Operand 2
	<>		IF Operand 1 is not equal to (e.g., it is less than or greater than) Operand 2

The operands specified in a conditional are either literals (constants) or variables. The operands used in the condition must be of the same type, meaning that string variables or literals can only be compared to other string variables or literals, and numeric variables can only be compared to numeric variables or literals. Here are examples of valid conditions using relational operators:

- IF TAX = .25 THEN . . .

- IF SALARY1 <> SALARY2 THEN . . .

- IF SALES >= 500.00 THEN . . .

- IF EMP.NAME$ = "Paul Newman" THEN . . .

Now consider these examples of invalid comparisons:

Examples of Invalid Comparisons	Reason Comparison Is Invalid
IF TAX = ".25" THEN . . .	TAX, a numeric variable, cannot be compared to ".25", a string constant.
IF CODE1 <> CODE2$ THEN . . .	CODE1, a numeric variable, cannot be compared to CODE2$, a string variable.
IF SALES$ >= 500.00 THEN . . .	SALES$, a string variable, cannot be compared to 500.00, a numeric constant.

The outcome of an IF statement depends on whether the condition is true or false. Consider the following IF statements. Note that the format for an IF statement in BASICA is *not* the same as it is for QBASIC:

- **QBASIC—Hours Test**

```
IF  Hours < 40 THEN
    PRINT "Overtime Pay Required"
ELSE
    PRINT "Regular Pay Only"
END IF
```

- **BASICA—Hours Test**

```
10  IF HOURS > 40 THEN PRINT "Overtime Pay Required"
    ELSE PRINT "Regular Pay Only"
```

With BASICA, an IF instruction, which is terminated when you press the Enter key, is limited to 255 characters.

With QBASIC, the structure of an IF statement is very much like pseudocode. IF-THEN-ELSE statements are *not* limited in length to 255 characters on a line as they are with BASICA. IF-THEN-ELSE statements are coded as follows in QBASIC. They always end with END IF.

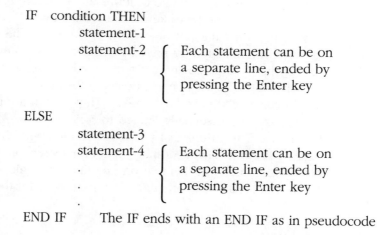

In QBASIC, each clause must go on a separate line and *no* line numbers should be used. With BASICA, the entire IF is coded on a single logical line, which can extend to 255 characters. (Later we will show you how to extend a line to 255 characters in BASICA.)

In either the QBASIC or BASICA Hours Test above, if the variable called HOURS has a value greater than 40 then the constant "Overtime Pay Required" is displayed. If HOURS is not greater than 40 (if it is <= 40), then the constant "Regular Pay Only" is displayed.

Thus, by using the IF statement, you test the initial condition; and if it is met or is "true" you perform the instruction(s) specified. By using ELSE, you can perform an operation or operations if the initial condition is not met or is "false." The ELSE clause is itself optional.

In pseudocode, an IF statement must end with a scope terminator of ENDIF to signal the end of the structure. This is coded as END IF in QBASIC. END IF is, however, not necessary in BASICA, which uses line numbers; that is, the IF instruction is coded with a line number and the computer understands that this IF, which may be coded on several lines, ends when the Enter key is pressed and a new line number is coded. Therefore, an IF statement may be coded on several lines, but only its first line is given a line number. Because the computer assumes the full IF structure is terminated when you press the Enter key, no END IF or scope terminator is used in BASICA.

Each clause is on a separate line with QBASIC. Note, however, that using separate physical lines for an IF-THEN-ELSE in BASICA requires special handling.

BASICA Restriction   Although you may code portions of the IF-THEN-ELSE structure on several lines in BASICA, the IF is actually just a single instruction with a single line number. Hence, pressing the Enter key at the end of each physical line in BASICA, which means the instruction is complete, will convey the wrong message to the computer. To tell the computer that you wish to end a line but *not* end the instruction, press the Ctrl key and, while it is still depressed, press the Enter key. We designate this as Ctrl + Enter; it tells the computer to continue the instruction on the next line. To end or terminate the entire instruction after the last ELSE statement, press the Enter key in the usual way.

Note that only the last line of the IF structure, the line prior to the next line number, is terminated by pressing the Enter key. The other lines are considered part of the IF structure and are terminated by pressing Ctrl + Enter.

Each BASICA instruction, regardless of the number of clauses it uses, is restricted to 255 characters (including blanks). Thus, if you are using an 80-column screen format, you are essentially limited to 3 lines (80 × 3) and a small portion of a fourth line. This means that you may need to condense your IF statements somewhat in BASICA. That is, if more than one instruction is to be executed if a given condition is met, put them all on one line, or at most two lines, separated by a colon (:). Similarly use one line, or at most two, for the ELSE clause.

- **BASICA**

```
IF ... THEN statement-1 : statement-2     'The entire instruction
ELSE statement-3 : statement-4            'can use a maximum
                                          'of 3 lines
```

All lines except the last end by pressing the Ctrl + Enter keys. If numerous statements are required when a condition is met, you have some flexibility but are still limited to three lines. For example,

- **BASICA**

```
10 IF AMT > 0 THEN PRINT "AMT IS POSITIVE" : TOTAL = TOTAL + 1: ─┐
        CTR = CTR + 1 ←Press Ctrl + Enter to end these lines ────┘
     ELSE PRINT "AMT <= 0" ←─── Press ENTER to end this line
```

BASICA Guidelines Indent CTR = CTR + 1 to indicate that it is part of the IF condition. The first two lines end by pressing Ctrl + Enter; the last line ends by pressing just the Enter key. Use colons to separate a series of instructions to be executed IF the condition is met or after the ELSE clause.

Later you will see that if numerous instructions are to be executed after the IF-THEN or after the ELSE, you can execute them as a separate module or subroutine. For now, code the IF-THEN on one or two lines and the ELSE on one or two lines, using colons (:) to separate instructions, but be sure that the full IF-THEN-ELSE does not exceed three lines.

The preferred format of coding each IF-THEN and ELSE on a separate line (terminated by pressing Ctrl + Enter) and indenting clauses within the IF and ELSE clauses, makes it easy to follow the structure of an IF statement. It also makes the program easier to read and to debug. Note, however, that this format does not affect the translation process. So, this coding technique is not a requirement, even though we strongly recommend it. Press the Tab to indent eight spaces.

More than one statement can be executed if the condition is true or is met; similarly within the ELSE clause, more than one statement can be executed if the condition is false or is not met. The following statements will perform two operations if WEIGHT is > 200 and two different operations if WEIGHT is not > 200:

- **Pseudocode**

```
IF   WEIGHT exceeds 200 THEN
        PRINT a message
        Add 1 to OVERWEIGHTCTR
ELSE
        PRINT a message
        Add 1 to OKWEIGHTCTR
ENDIF
```

- **QBASIC program excerpt**

```
IF   WEIGHT > 200 THEN
     PRINT "Diet"
     OVERWEIGHTCTR = OVERWEIGHTCTR + 1
ELSE
     PRINT "OK Weight"
     OKWEIGHTCTR = OKWEIGHTCTR + 1
END IF
```

- **BASICA program excerpt**

```
10 IF WEIGHT > 200 THEN PRINT "Diet":OVERWEIGHTCTR = OVERWEIGHTCTR + 1
   ELSE PRINT "OK Weight" : OKWEIGHTCTR = OKWEIGHTCTR + 1
20 ...
```

Example 1

The following pseudocode plans a program that inputs sales amounts and, for each, calculates and prints a commission. If a sales amount is less than $500.00, the commission is 5 percent. Otherwise the commission is 10 percent.

- **Pseudocode**

```
START
     Input Sales Amount
     WHILE there is still input
          IF   Sales Amount is less than $500.00 THEN
               Commission is 5% of Sales Amount
          ELSE
               Commission is 10% of Sales Amount
          ENDIF
          Print Commission
          Input Sales Amount
     WEND
STOP
```

The full QBASIC and BASICA programs to calculate and print the commission follow:

- **QBASIC Program**

```
'This program calculates and prints commission
PRINT "Enter Sales Amount - Type 99999 When Done"
INPUT SALES.AMOUNT
WHILE SALES.AMOUNT < 99999
    IF  SALES.AMOUNT < 500 THEN
        COMMISSION = .05 * SALES.AMOUNT
    ELSE
        COMMISSION = .10 * SALES.AMOUNT
    END IF
        PRINT "Commission is "; COMMISSION
        INPUT SALES.AMOUNT
WEND
END
```

- **BASICA Program**

```
10   'This program calculates and prints commission
20   PRINT "Enter Sales Amount - Type 99999 When Done"
30   INPUT SALES.AMOUNT
40   WHILE SALES.AMOUNT < 99999
50      IF  SALES.AMOUNT < 500 THEN   'Press Ctrl+Enter at end of line
             COMMISSION = .05 * SALES.AMOUNT   'Press Ctrl+Enter
          ELSE COMMISSION = .10 * SALES.AMOUNT   'Press Enter
60      PRINT "Commission is "; COMMISSION
70      INPUT SALES.AMOUNT
80   WEND
90   END
```

Example 2

The following pseudocode plans a program that will print the average salaries of males and females. The sex and salary for each employee in the company will be entered as input on a single line.

- **Pseudocode**

```
START
        Initialize Counters and Totals
        Input Sex and Salary
        WHILE there is still input
              IF   Sex is Female THEN
                      Add 1 to Female Counter
                      Add Salary to Total Female Salaries
              ELSE
                      Add 1 to Male Counter
                      Add Salary to Total Male Salaries
              ENDIF
              INPUT Sex and Salary
        WEND
        Calculate and Print Average Female Salary
        Calculate and Print Average Male Salary
STOP
```

The full QBASIC and BASICA programs to print the average salaries for males and females follow:

- **QBASIC program**

```
'This program calculates average salaries for males and females
FEMALECTR = 0
MALECTR = 0
```

```
TOTFEMALESALARIES = 0
TOTMALESALS = 0
PRINT "Enter Sex (M, F) and Salary"
PRINT "Enter 9, 999999 when done"
INPUT SEX$, SALARY
WHILE SEX$ <> "9"
    IF  SEX$ = "F" THEN
        FEMALECTR = FEMALECTR + 1
        TOTFEMALESALARIES = TOTFEMALESALARIES + SALARY
    ELSE
        MALECTR = MALECTR + 1
        TOTMALESALS = TOTMALESALS + SALARY
    END IF
    INPUT SEX, SALARY
WEND
AVERAGEFEMALESALARY = TOTFEMALESALARIES / FEMALECTR
AVERAGEMALESALARY = TOTMALESALS / MALECTR
PRINT "The Average Salary for Females is "; AVERAGEFEMALESALARY
PRINT "The Average Salary for Males is "; AVERAGEMALESALARY
END
```

• **Run** (press Ctrl + F5 in QBASIC or F2 in BASICA)

```
Enter Sex (M, F) and Salary
Enter 9, 999999 when done
? M, 1000
? F, 500
? F, 500
? M, 1000
? 9, 999999
The Average Salary for Females is 500
The Average Salary for Males is 1000
```

• **BASICA program**

```
10 'This program calculates average salaries for males and females
20 FEMALECTR = 0
30 MALECTR = 0
40 TOTFEMALESALARIES = 0
50 TOTMALESALS = 0
60 PRINT "Enter Sex (M, F) and Salary"
70 PRINT "Enter 9, 999999 when done"
80 INPUT SEX$, SALARY
90 WHILE SEX$ <> "9"
100    IF SEX$ = "F" THEN FEMALECTR = FEMALECTR + 1 :
           TOTFEMALESALARIES = TOTFEMALESALARIES + SALARY
         ELSE MALECTR = MALECTR + 1:TOTMALESALS = TOTMALESALS + SALARY
```

```
110    INPUT SEX$, SALARY
120 WEND
130 AVERAGEFEMALESALARY = TOTFEMALESALARIES / FEMALECTR
140 AVERAGEMALESALARY = TOTMALESALS / MALECTR
150 PRINT "The Average Salary for Females is "; AVERAGEFEMALESALARY
160 PRINT "The Average Salary for Males is "; AVERAGEMALESALARY
170 END
```

- **Run** (press Ctrl + F5 in QBASIC or F2 in BASICA)

```
Enter Sex (M, F) and Salary
Enter 9, 999999 when done
? M, 1000
? F, 500
? F, 500
? M, 1000
? 9, 999999
The Average Salary for Females is 500
The Average Salary for Males is 1000
```

Self-test

Plan each of the following programs with pseudocode first.

1. Write a program to input a series of Employee Names with their Gross Pay, each on a single line. For each employee, calculate Federal Income Tax as 20 percent of Gross Pay if the employee earns less than $50,000. Otherwise the Federal Income Tax rate is 25 percent. Print each employees's name and the Federal Income Tax owed.
2. Write a program to input employee names and salaries, each on a single line. Give employees who earn 25000 or less a 10 percent bonus, and give employees who earn more than 25000 an 8 percent bonus. Print each employee's name and bonus. At the end of the run, print the sum of all bonuses that the company will pay.

Solutions

1. Pseudocode:

> START
> > Input Name and Gross Pay
> > WHILE there is still input
> > > IF   Gross Pay < 50000 THEN
> > > > Federal Tax is 20% of Gross Pay
> > > ELSE
> > > > Federal Tax is 25% of Gross Pay
> > > ENDIF
> > > Print Name and Federal Tax

Input Name and Gross Pay
WEND
STOP

QBASIC program:

```
'This program calculates federal income tax
PRINT "Enter Name and Gross Pay"
PRINT "Type Stop, 999999 when done"
INPUT EMPNAME$, GROSSPAY
WHILE GROSSPAY < 999999
    IF  GROSSPAY < 50000 THEN
        FEDLTAX = .20 * GROSSPAY
    ELSE
        FEDLTAX = .25 * GROSSPAY
    END IF
    LPRINT EMPNAME$; " owes "; FEDLTAX
    INPUT EMPNAME$, GROSSPAY
WEND
END
```

BASICA program:

```
10   'This program calculates federal income tax
20   PRINT "Enter Name and Gross Pay "
30   PRINT "Type Stop, 999999 when done"
40   INPUT EMPNAME$, GROSSPAY
50   WHILE GROSSPAY < 999999
60       IF  GROSSPAY < 50000 THEN FEDLTAX = .20 * GROSSPAY
                ELSE FEDLTAX = .25 * GROSSPAY
70       LPRINT EMPNAME$; " owes "; FEDLTAX
80       INPUT EMPNAME$, GROSSPAY
90   WEND
100  END
```

2. Pseudocode:

START
Enter Name and Salary
Initialize Total Bonus
WHILE Salary > 0
IF   Salary <= 25000 THEN
Bonus is 10% of Salary
ELSE
Bonus is 8% of Salary

                    ENDIF
                    Print Name and Bonus
                    Add Bonus to Total Bonus
                    Enter Name and Salary
                WEND
                Print Total Bonus
            STOP

QBASIC program:

```
'This program prints bonuses and calculates total bonuses paid
TOTAL.BONUS = 0
PRINT "Enter Name and Salary"
PRINT "Type END, 0 When Done"
INPUT EMPNAME$, SALARY
WHILE SALARY > 0
    IF  SALARY <= 25000 THEN
        BONUS = .10 * SALARY
    ELSE
        BONUS = .08 * SALARY
    END IF
    LPRINT "Bonus for "; EMPNAME$;" is "; BONUS
    TOTAL.BONUS = TOTAL.BONUS + BONUS
    INPUT EMPNAME$, SALARY
WEND
LPRINT "Total Bonus is "; TOTAL.BONUS
END
```

BASICA program:

```
10   'This program prints bonuses and calculates total bonuses paid
20   TOTAL.BONUS = 0
30   PRINT "Enter Name and Salary"
40   PRINT "Type END, 0 When Done"
50   INPUT EMPNAME$, SALARY
60   WHILE SALARY > 0
70       IF  SALARY <= 25000 THEN BONUS = .10 * SALARY
         ELSE
             BONUS = .08 * SALARY
80       LPRINT "Bonus for "; EMPNAME$;" is "; BONUS
90       TOTAL.BONUS = TOTAL.BONUS + BONUS
100      INPUT EMPNAME$, SALARY
110  WEND
120  LPRINT "Total Bonus is "; TOTAL.BONUS
130  END
```

How Comparisons Are Performed

In BASIC, numeric comparisons are performed algebraically, but string comparisons follow a different set of rules, as you will learn in the following sections.

Comparing Numeric Variables When comparing numeric variables, the following are all considered equal:

$$012 \qquad 12.00 \qquad 12 \qquad +12$$

That is, numeric comparisons are performed in BASIC algebraically. Thus, the number of digits being compared in numeric operands will not affect the comparison. The number $001 = 01 = 1$ even though each value has a different number of digits. Moreover, positive numbers are recognized as equal to unsigned numbers.

Comparing String Operands The number of characters in string variables always affects the comparison. Also, string variables are compared alphabetically so that "ABC" < "BBC" < "ZBC". But how would "ABC" be compared to "ABCD"?

If two string variables being compared are of unequal length but have equal values up to the length of the shorter one, then the shorter string operand is considered less than the longer one regardless of the rightmost characters in the longer string. Consider the following examples of comparing string data.

$$\text{``ABC''} < \text{``ABCD''}$$
$$\text{``DOG''} < \text{``DOGS''}$$
$$\text{``DOG ''} < \text{``DOG   ''}$$
$$\text{``tes''} < \text{``test''}$$

If a shorter string has the same leftmost characters as a longer string, as in these examples, the shorter is considered < the longer.

A string variable can be assigned a value such as "DOG" by coding LET X\$ = "DOG", or it can be assigned the same value by coding INPUT X\$. During the run, the user could input DOG or "DOG" in response to the ? prompt. To input rightmost or leftmost blanks, such as " DOG" or "DOG   ", in place of simply "DOG", the user must key in quotation marks around the value as indicated—for example, "DOG   " instead of "DOG".

As a rule, when comparing string operands of different lengths, the number of characters compared is determined by the size of the shorter string.

String operands are not compared algebraically as are numeric operands. That is, "123" is greater than "0123" because the high-order, or leading, "1" is greater than the high-order "0." This is true even though a numeric variable with contents 123 would be considered equal to a numeric variable with contents 0123. Similarly " abc" is considered less than "abc" because the first operand has a high-order, or leftmost, blank.

The ASCII Collating Sequence

When performing an alphanumeric comparison, the hierarchy of the comparison, called the **collating sequence**, is determined by the computer.

The internal code that is most commonly used for representing data in microcomputers is ASCII, an abbreviation for American Standard Code for Information Interchange. Characters are compared to one another in ASCII as shown in Figure 8.1.

On ASCII computers, a numeric comparison is performed properly, as noted; that is, the number 012 is less than 022, which is less than 042, and so on. Uppercase and lowercase alphabetic comparisons are also performed properly. Thus the computer is able to determine if data is arranged alphabetically because "A" is considered less than "B", which is less than "C", and so on. Thus, "ABDC" < "BBCD" < "XBCD", and so on. Similarly, "a" < "b" < "c" . . . < "z".

Note, however, that on ASCII computers uppercase letters are considered less than lowercase letters, so that "A" < "a", "Z" < "z", "TEST" < "test", and so on. Thus, if uppercase and lowercase letters are mixed when entering data or when assigning a string value to a string variable, a comparison could produce unexpected results. Consider the following examples of comparing mixed uppercase and lowercase letters:

"ABC" < "abc"

"Abc" < "abc"

"ZIP" < "apple"

"ZIP" < "ZIp"

When entering a value for a string variable or using an assignment statement to assign a value to a string variable, use either all uppercase letters, all lowercase

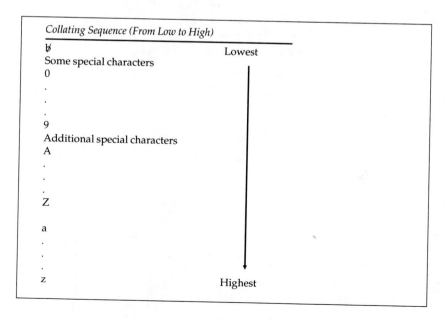

Figure 8.1
ASCII collating sequence.

letters, or an initial uppercase letter followed by all lowercase letters. In this way, you will minimize the risk of erroneous processing when string operands are compared. The functions UCASE$ and LCASE$ can change strings into either all uppercase or all lowercase. These functions keep case differences from affecting a comparison. You can, for example, make the contents of a variable called CODE$ all uppercase by coding LET CODE$ = UCASE$(CODE$). This ensures that CODE$ contains all uppercase letters.

Note, too, that, on ASCII computers, numbers are less than letters, so that "ROUTE 109," for example, in an address variable is greater than "100 MAIN ST" because the first character, R, compares "greater than" the number 1.

If you are using an IBM mainframe version of BASIC, the collating sequence for your computer may be EBCDIC rather than ASCII. EBCDIC, an abbreviation for Extended Binary Coded Decimal Interchange Code, is the other main computer code for representing data, but it is used mostly on IBM mainframes. In EBCDIC's collating sequence, letters are less than numbers and uppercase letters are less than lowercase letters.

Self-test

1. What is wrong with the following IF statement in QBASIC?

```
IF  AMT = 0
     PRINT "Amt Is Zero"
END IF
```

2. Write a routine to move the smallest of three numbers AMT1, AMT2, and AMT3 to a variable called PRINTSMALL and print it.

For questions 3 through 5, indicate the results if the groups of two literals are compared:
3. "IBM"   "ibm"
4. "BASIC"   "BASICA"
5. "123"   123
6. Write a BASIC program to input per line a Name, Hours worked, and Code. If the code = 1, the rate of pay is 5.00; if the code = 2, the rate of pay is 7.00; and if the code = 3, the rate of pay is 10.00. Print Name and Wages for each input line. First plan the program with pseudocode.

Solutions

1. The word THEN is missing from the first line of the IF statement.
2. QBASIC routine:

```
PRINTSMALL = AMT1
IF  AMT2 < PRINTSMALL THEN
     PRINTSMALL = AMT2
END IF
```

```
IF  AMT3 < PRINTSMALL THEN
     PRINTSMALL = AMT3
END IF
PRINT PRINTSMALL
```

BASICA routine:

```
10  PRINTSMALL = AMT1
20  IF  AMT2 < PRINTSMALL THEN        'Press Ctrl+Enter keys
          PRINTSMALL = AMT2           'Press Enter key
30  IF  AMT3 < PRINTSMALL THEN        'Press Ctrl+Enter keys
          PRINTSMALL = AMT3           'Press Enter key
40  PRINT PRINTSMALL
```

3. "IBM" < "ibm" (uppercase is < lowercase)
4. "BASIC" < "BASICA" (shorter string < longer string if strings are equal up to length of the shorter string)
5. This comparison is not valid because string variables and numeric variables cannot be compared. To do so will cause a syntax error.
6. Pseudocode:

```
            START
                 Enter Name, Hours and Code
                 WHILE there is still input
                      Initialize Rate
                      IF  Code = 1 THEN
                           Rate = 5.00
                      ENDIF
                      IF  Code = 2 THEN
                           Rate = 7.00
                      ENDIF
                      IF  Code = 3 THEN
                           Rate = 10.00
                      ENDIF
                      Calculate Wages
                      Print Wages
                      Enter Name, Hours and Code
                 WEND
            STOP
```

QBASIC program:

```
'This program computes wages for employees
PRINT "Enter Name, Hours and Code"
PRINT "Type End, 99, 9 when done"
```

```
INPUT EMPNAME$, HOURS, CODE
WHILE CODE <> 9
    RATE = 0
    IF  CODE = 1 THEN
        RATE = 5.00
    END IF
    IF  CODE = 2 THEN
        RATE = 7.00
    END IF
    IF  CODE = 3 THEN
        RATE = 10.00
    END IF
    WAGES = HOURS * RATE
    PRINT EMPNAME$; " earned "; WAGES
    INPUT EMPNAME$, HOURS, CODE
WEND
END
```

BASICA program:

```
10   'This program computes wages for employees
20   PRINT "Enter Name, Hours and Code"
30   PRINT "Type End, 99, 9 when done"
40   INPUT EMPNAME$, HOURS, CODE
50   WHILE CODE <> 9
60       RATE = 0
70       IF  CODE = 1 THEN
             RATE = 5.00
80       IF  CODE = 2 THEN
             RATE = 7.00
90       IF  CODE = 3 THEN
             RATE = 10.00
100      WAGES = HOURS * RATE
110      PRINT EMPNAME$; " earned "; WAGES
120      INPUT EMPNAME$, HOURS, CODE
130  WEND
140  END
```

Nested Conditional

A **nested conditional** is a conditional in which an IF statement can itself contain additional IF clauses. Consider the following examples.

IF ... THEN IF ... As a Nested Conditional
One format for nested conditionals follows:

- **BASICA**

```
IF  condition-1 THEN IF condition-2 THEN statement-1
    ELSE statement-2
ELSE statement-3
```

- **QBASIC**

```
IF  condition-1 THEN
    IF  condition-2 THEN
            statement-1
    ELSE
            statement-2
    END IF
ELSE
        statement-3
END IF
```

Example

- **QBASIC**

```
IF  DEPT = 1 THEN
    IF  HOURS > 40 THEN
        BONUS = 3 * HOURS
    ELSE BONUS = 2 * HOURS
    END IF 'Each IF needs an END IF
ELSE BONUS = 0
END IF
PRINT BONUS
```

Note that with QBASIC the word THEN must be on the same line as the IF, and each IF clause must be delimited with an END IF.

- **BASICA**

```
10  IF  DEPT = 1 THEN IF HOURS > 40 THEN BONUS = 3 * HOURS
        ELSE BONUS = 2 * HOURS
    ELSE BONUS = 0
20  PRINT BONUS
```

This example in QBASIC and BASICA conforms to the original format specified for an IF instruction, but if the first condition specified is true, then another test is performed. This is one type of nested conditional. The tests performed are listed next:

1. If DEPT is not equal to 1, the last ELSE is executed, and BONUS is then set equal to 0.

2. If DEPT = 1, the second condition is tested as follows:

   - (If DEPT = 1) and HOURS is greater than 40, BONUS is set equal to 3 * HOURS.

   - (If DEPT = 1) and HOURS is not greater than 40, the first ELSE clause is executed and BONUS is set equal to 2 * HOURS.

The use of an indented clause helps to interpret the structure of the nested conditional. Be sure that the full instruction, however, does not exceed 255 characters when using BASICA.

A nested conditional is really a shortcut method of writing a series of simple conditionals. Thus, any nested conditional may be written instead with simple conditionals. In BASICA, each line in the example except the last is terminated by pressing Ctrl + Enter; only the last line is terminated by pressing the Enter key. With QBASIC, all lines are terminated by pressing the Enter key.

IF . . . THEN . . . ELSE IF . . . As a Nested Conditional

Another format for nested conditionals follows:

- **BASICA**

```
IF  condition-1 THEN statement-1
    ELSE IF  condition-2 THEN statement-2
ELSE statement-3
```

- **QBASIC**

```
IF  condition-1 THEN
    statement-1
ELSEIF condition-2 THEN
    statement-2
ELSE
    statement-3        Each clause can be on a separate line
END IF
```

- **BASICA** (press Ctrl + Enter at the end of the first 2 lines, then Enter at the end of the third line)

```
10  IF SALARY > 99999 THEN PRINT "Six Figure Salary"
        ELSE IF SALARY > 60000 THEN PRINT "Salary Between 60000 and 99999"
    ELSE PRINT "Salary Less Than or Equal to 60000"
```

BASICA Restriction When coding a nested conditional, as with any conditional, use at least one line for each IF or ELSE clause in the statement as long as you do not exceed three lines; indent where possible; use Ctrl + Enter when ending a clause within the statement and use the Enter key to terminate the entire statement; and be sure the instruction does not exceed 255 characters. (Recall that these special coding rules for IF statements apply to BASICA only.)

Self-test

1. A store that sells VCRs is having a sale; the color of the price tag indicates the discount on that item.

Color	Code	Discount
Red	R	30%
Green	G	25%
Blue	B	20%

Write a program that reads in the color code and the list price and then outputs the selling price. Use nested conditionals.

2. Use an IF statement to code the following: Enter, on each line, Student Name and NoOfCredits. If NoOfCredits is 12 or less, then the Tuition is $200 × NoOfCredits. If NoOfCredits is 13–15, the tuition is a flat $2600; if NoOfCredits is 16–18 the tuition is a flat $3200. Print an error message if NoOfCredits is in excess of 18. Use nested conditionals.

Solutions

1. QBASIC program:

```
PRINT "Enter Code (R, G, or B) and Price"
PRINT "Enter X, 0 to Exit"
INPUT Code$, Price
WHILE Code$ <> "X"
    IF   Code$ = "R" THEN
        Discount = .30
    ELSEIF Code$ = "G" THEN
        Discount = .25
    ELSEIF Code$ = "B" THEN
        Discount = .20
    ELSE
        PRINT "No discount"
        Discount = 0
    END IF
    SellingPrice = Price - Price * Discount
    PRINT "Selling Price is "; SellingPrice
    INPUT Code$, Price
WEND
PRINT "End of Program"
END
```

BASICA program:

```
10   PRINT "Enter Code (R, G, or B) and Price"
20   PRINT "Enter X, 0 to Exit"
30   INPUT CODE$,PRICE
40   WHILE CODE$ <> "X"
50      IF  CODE$ = "R" THEN DIS = .30 ELSE IF CODE$ = "G"
        THEN DIS = .25 ELSE IF CODE$ = "B" THEN DIS = .20
        ELSE PRINT "No discount" : DIS = 0
60      SELLINGPRICE = PRICE - PRICE * DIS
70      PRINT "Selling Price is "; SELLINGPRICE
80      INPUT CODE$, PRICE
90   WEND
100  PRINT "End of Program"
110  END
```

2. QBASIC program:

```
PRINT "Enter Student Name and Number of Credits"
PRINT "Enter STOP, 99 when done"
INPUT StudName$, NoOfCredits
WHILE  NoOfCredits < 99
    IF  NoOfCredits <= 12 THEN
        Tuition = NoOfCredits * 200
        ELSEIF NoOfCredits < 16 THEN
            Tuition = 2600
            ELSEIF  NoOfCredits < 19 THEN
                Tuition = 3200
                ELSE
                    Tuition = 0
    END IF
    PRINT "Tuition for "; StudName$; " is "; Tuition
    INPUT StudName$, NoOfCredits
WEND
```

BASICA program:

```
10   PRINT "Enter Student Name and Number of Credits"
20   PRINT "Enter STOP, 99 when done"
30   INPUT STUDNAME$, CREDITS
40   WHILE CREDITS < 99
50      IF CREDITS <= 12 THEN TUITION = CREDITS * 200
            ELSE IF CREDITS < 16 THEN TUITION = 2600
            ELSE IF CREDITS < 19 THEN TUITION = 3200 ELSE TUITION = 0
60   PRINT "Tuition for "; STUDNAME$; " is "; TUITION
```

```
70  INPUT STUDNAME$, CREDITS
80  WEND
90  END
```

With QBASIC there should be no line numbers and each clause in the IF statement can, and should, be on a separate line. The entire IF ends with END IF.

Compound Conditional

We have seen that the selection structure provides programs with a great deal of logical control capability. The **compound conditional** provides even greater flexibility for selection and enables the IF statement to be used for more complex problems. With the compound conditional, the programmer can test for several conditions in a single IF-THEN-ELSE structure.

OR in a Compound Conditional

To perform an operation or a series of operations if any one of several conditions is met, a compound conditional with conditions separated by OR is used. This means that if any one of several conditions is met, the statement(s) specified is executed:

IF   condition-1 OR condition-2 THEN . . .

As in all conditionals, the ELSE IF and the ELSE clauses may be used, but they are optional. Review these examples:

- **QBASIC**

```
1. IF  AMT1 < AMT3 OR AMT1 = AMT4 THEN
       LET TOTAL = TOTAL + AMT1
   ELSE
       LET TOTAL = 0
   END IF
2. IF  SEX$ = "M" OR SEX$ = "F" THEN
       PRINT "Sex Code Is Correct"
   END IF
```

- **BASICA**

```
1. 10  IF  AMT1 < AMT3 OR AMT1 = AMT4 THEN
           LET TOTAL = TOTAL + AMT1
       ELSE LET TOTAL = 0
2. 10  IF  SEX$ = "M" OR SEX$ = "F" THEN
           PRINT "Sex Code Is Correct"
```

By using OR in a compound conditional, if any of the conditions is true, execution of the statement(s) specified will occur. If none of the conditions is met, the computer executes either the ELSE or ELSEIF clause, if used, or the statement on the next line number. Any number of conditions separated by ORs may be specified in a single statement.

In the first example, TOTAL is set equal to 0 only if AMT1 is greater than or equal to AMT3 *and* AMT1 is not equal to AMT4. If *either* AMT1 is less than AMT3, *or* AMT1 is equal to AMT4, AMT1 will be added to TOTAL and then the statement on the next line number will be executed.

In the second example, recall that string constants being compared to string variables must be enclosed in quotes.

Keep in mind that each condition must include operands of the same type. Separate conditions may, however, include either a string or numeric comparison:

```
IF  DEPT = 1 OR LOCATION$ = "New York" THEN
    PRINT "Attend the meeting"
END IF  ←Required with QBASIC
```

BASICA Restriction As with any conditional in BASICA, only the first line has a line number. Use Ctrl + Enter to terminate all lines until the last, which is terminated by pressing the Enter key. Be sure that the instruction does not exceed 255 characters.

AND in a Compound Conditional

If a statement or statements are to be executed only when all of several conditions are met, use AND in the compound conditional, as in IF condition-1 AND condition-2 . . . THEN . . . . All conditions must be met when AND is used in a compound conditional. The ELSE or ELSEIF option (if specified) will be performed if any one of the stated conditions is not met.

For example, suppose you want to print "This is a male under 6 ft and < 200 lb" if all of the following conditions are met:

Sex$ = "M"; Height less than 72 inches; Weight less than 200 pounds

Otherwise, you want to print "This person does not meet all three conditions". In other words, if one or more of these conditions are not met, you want to print the latter phrase. You can use a compound conditional for this:

```
IF  SEX$ = "M" AND HEIGHT < 72 AND WEIGHT < 200 THEN
    PRINT "This is a male under 6 ft and < 200 lb"
ELSE
    PRINT "This person does not meet all three conditions"
END IF  ←Required with QBASIC
```

The ELSE clause is executed in the preceding if *any one* of the specified conditions is not met.

Using Both AND and OR in the Same Statement

You can use both AND and OR in a single compound conditional. For example:

```
IF  SEX$ = "F" OR SEX$ = "M" AND AGE > 25 THEN
    PRINT "Regular Insuree"
ELSE
    PRINT "Assigned Risk"
END IF  ←Required with QBASIC
```

When using both AND and OR in the same compound conditional, the order of evaluation of each condition tested is critical. Consider these parts of the statement:

```
    (1) SEX$ = "F" OR SEX$ = "M"
AND (2) AGE > 25
```

In this case, "Regular Insuree" prints if (1) SEX$ is "F" or "M", *and* (2) AGE > 25. That is, any male or female who is over 25 years old is considered a Regular Insuree. Alternatively, for anyone who is 25 or under, "Assigned Risk" prints.

Suppose, however, that this IF statement is evaluated in the following order:

```
   (1) SEX$ = "F"
OR (2) SEX$ = "M" AND AGE > 25
```

If this is the order of evaluation, then "Regular Insuree" prints for females *or* males over 25 years old.

The following hierarchy rules indicate how orders of evaluation are actually used:

- Conditions surrounding the word AND are evaluated first.

- Conditions surrounding the word OR are evaluated last.

- When there are several AND or OR connectors, the AND conditions are evaluated first, as they appear in the statement, from left to right. Then the OR conditions are evaluated, also from left to right.

- To override rules 1 through 3, use parentheses around conditions to be evaluated first.

Now let us use these hierarchy rules to evaluate the example. "Regular Insuree" prints if:

```
   (1) SEX$ = "F"
OR (2) SEX$ = "M" AND AGE > 25
```

This is the same as the second order of evaluation specified above.

To change the order so that the hierarchy rules are overridden, use parentheses. As a general rule, to simplify coding, to minimize errors, and to clarify a program, it is best to use parentheses in a compound conditional with ANDs and ORs even if they are not required.

You can test for values of a variable between two endpoints. For example, let us print the literal "It fits!" for values of AMT1 between 10 and 13 inclusive of the endpoints. "Inclusive of the endpoints" means including the values 10 and 13:

```
IF  AMT1 >= 10 AND AMT1 <= 13 THEN
    PRINT "It fits!"
END IF
```

This is the most efficient method for coding the program excerpt correctly.

Negating Conditionals

All relational operators can be negated:

$$\text{IF NOT condition THEN}$$

.
.
.

Example

Negating a Simple Conditional	Alternative Coding
IF NOT AMT < 7	(same as IF AMT >= 7)
IF NOT AMT > 7	(same as IF AMT <= 7)

The following two statements, then, are equivalent:

- Statement (a)

```
IF  AMT >= 0 THEN
    PRINT "AMT is zero or positive"
ELSE
    PRINT "AMT is negative"
END IF  ←Required with QBASIC
```

- Statement (b)

```
IF  NOT AMT < 0 THEN
    PRINT "AMT is zero or positive"
ELSE
    PRINT "AMT is negative"
END IF  ←Required with QBASIC
```

In all instances, the word NOT follows the word IF and precedes the condition to be tested. That is, code IF NOT AMT = 7 THEN .... Coding IF AMT NOT = 7 would cause a syntax error.

As a rule, it is easier to read and walk through a program that tests if a condition is true rather than using a NOT to test if a condition is false.

Self-test

1. What, if anything, is wrong with the following QBASIC statement? Correct the errors.

```
IF  A < 21  OR  A = 21  AND  A = 5  OR  A > 5  THEN
    PRINT "A OK"
END IF
```

2. Write a single statement to print "A OK" if A is between 10 and 20, inclusive of the endpoints.

3. Find the absolute value of A. (The absolute value of a number is its distance from 0 regardless of sign. The absolute value of 3 is 3; the absolute value of −3 is 3.)

4. Determine if a string variable called Code$ contains numeric data.

5. Calculate weekly wages based on input values of hourly rate and hours worked. For employees who have worked more than 40 hours, pay them time-and-a-half for overtime. An hours worked figure of 99 denotes the end of the job. Plan your program first using pseudocode.

6. A certain club will only admit members who are 21 years old or older. In addition, all members must either have an income of more than $40,000 or an available credit line of at least $5000. Write an IF-THEN-ELSE statement to reflect the club membership's selection criteria.

7. Write an IF-THEN-ELSE statement for the following problem. If your year-end bonus is more than $2500 and your outstanding bills are less than $2000, then display "Go On Vacation" on the screen; otherwise display "Stay Home This Year".

Solutions

1. There should be parentheses around conditions to make the statement logical:

```
IF  (A < 21 OR A = 21)  AND  (A = 5 OR A > 5) THEN
    PRINT "A OK"
END IF
```

2. ```
IF A <= 20 AND A >= 10 THEN
    PRINT "A OK"
END IF
```
```

3. QBASIC:

```
IF  A >= 0 THEN
    PRINT "Absolute Value of "; A; " is "; A
ELSE
    PRINT "Absolute Value of "; A; " is "; -1 * A
END IF
```

4. BASICA:

```
IF Code$ > "9" OR Code$ < "0" THEN PRINT Code$;" IS NOT NUMERIC"
ELSE PRINT Code$; " IS NUMERIC"
```

5. Pseudocode:

```
START
        INPUT Hourly Rate and Hours Worked
        WHILE Hours Worked <> 99
                IF   Hours Worked <= 40 THEN
                        Wages = Hours Worked * Hourly Rate
                ELSE
                        Wages = 40 * Hourly Rate + (Hours Worked -
                                40) * (Hourly Rate * 1.5)
                ENDIF
                PRINT Wages
                INPUT Hourly Rate and Hours Worked
        WEND
    STOP
```

QBASIC program:

```
PRINT "Enter Rate and Hours - Type 99,99 when Done"
INPUT HourlyRate, HoursWorked
WHILE HoursWorked <> 99
    IF  HoursWorked <= 40 THEN
        Wages = HoursWorked * HourlyRate
    ELSE
        RegularWages = 40 * HoursWorked
        OvertimeWages = (HoursWorked - 40) * (HourlyRate * 1.5)
        Wages = RegularWages + OvertimeWages
    END IF
    PRINT Wages
    INPUT HourlyRate, HoursWorked
WEND
END
```

BASICA program:

```
10   PRINT "Enter Rate and Hours - Type 99,99 when Done"
20   INPUT HOURLYRATE, HOURS
30   WHILE HOURS <> 99
40       IF  HOURS <= 40 THEN WAGES = HOURS * HOURLYRATE
         ELSE REGULARWAGES = 40 * HOURLYRATE:OVERTIMEWAGES = (HOURS - 40) *
              (HOURLYRATE * 1.5):WAGES = REGULARWAGES + OVERTIMEWAGES
50       PRINT WAGES
60       INPUT HOURLYRATE, HOURS
70   WEND
80   END
```

6. With compound conditionals:

QBASIC:

```
IF  AGE >= 21 AND (INCOME > 40000 OR CREDIT >= 5000) THEN
    PRINT "Meets Criteria"
ELSE
    PRINT "Does Not Meet Criteria"
END IF
```

With nested conditionals:

BASICA:

```
10   IF  AGE < 21 THEN PRINT "Does Not Meet Criteria"
     ELSE IF INCOME > 40000 OR CREDIT >= 5000 THEN PRINT "Meets Criteria"
     ELSE PRINT "Does Not Meet Criteria"
```

7. BASICA statement:

```
10   IF  YEAR.END.BONUS > 2500 AND OUTSTANDING.BILLS < 2000 THEN
         PRINT "Go On Vacation"
     ELSE PRINT "Stay Home This Year"
```

9

Iteration, Looping, and Subroutines for Logical Control and Top-Down Programming

Recall that there are four logical control structures used in all programs regardless of the programming language:

Logical Control Structure	Meaning
Sequence	Program steps are executed in the order they appear.
Selection	An IF-THEN-ELSE selects the instruction or instructions to be executed, depending on whether or not a condition is met.
Iteration	A series of steps is executed repeatedly; continued execution is based on whether or not a given condition or conditions are met.
Case	One of a number of steps is executed depending on the contents of a variable or variables.

In this section we focus specifically on iteration, or looping. We will provide additional information on the WHILE . . . WEND and then discuss other iterative techniques.

Iterative Techniques

The WHILE . . . WEND loop, nested iterations, and FOR . . . NEXT statements are types of iterative techniques.

More on the WHILE . . . WEND Loop for Iteration

A WHILE (condition) . . . WEND is executed repeatedly until the condition specified is no longer true or met. When the loop is terminated, execution of the program continues with the statement following the word WEND. WHILE . . . WEND is used for iteration in BASICA and QBASIC; other versions of BASIC may use different delimiters, such as DO WHILE . . . LOOP (VAX), WHILE . . . NEXT, and the like. All, however, are used in the same way for looping.

If the condition tested in the WHILE . . . WEND is not met initially, the loop is not executed at all. Note that the test for the specified condition is made even before the series of steps is executed even once.

Consider the following loop:

```
WHILE AMT1 <> 9999
    .
    .
    .

WEND
```

Suppose AMT1 is entered initially as 9999, meaning that there are no valid AMT1 variables at all. Before the statements within the WHILE . . . WEND are executed, AMT1 is compared with 9999. Since AMT1 equals 9999 at the beginning, the condition in the WHILE loop is not met, even initially. In this case, the statements within the WHILE . . . WEND are not executed at all. Thus, program execution would continue with the statement following WEND. This is the correct procedure because if a trailer value is entered initially, then there is no valid data to process and you would want to bypass the loop entirely.

Repeating, or iterating, a series of steps any number of times as in the above example is called *looping*. We used WHILE AMT1 <> 9999 because we had an unknown number of input variables to process; in such cases, a trailer value is entered to force the WHILE . . . WEND to terminate. The trailer value is entered after all "real" input, regardless of the actual number of input variables to be processed.

Sometimes, however, you know in advance the exact number of times you want to execute a loop. In such cases you can use a counter along with a WHILE . . . WEND to control the number of times a procedure is repeated. Instead of testing for a trailer value to terminate the loop, the WHILE statement tests the counter to see if the loop has been executed the required number of times.

For example, you can use a counter to process a fixed number of variables. Suppose you input customer data as follows:

> Customer Name
> Street Address
> City State Zip   (assume no commas between City, State, and Zip)

The following program will print one mailing label for each of 25 customers:

```
PRINT "Enter Name on Line 1, Street Address on Line 2"
PRINT "Enter City State Zip on Line 3"
LET LABEL.CTR = 0
    INPUT CUST.NAME$
```

```
      INPUT ST.ADDR$
      INPUT CITY.STATE.ZIP$
WHILE LABEL.CTR < 25
      LPRINT CUST.NAME$
      LPRINT ST.ADDR$
      LPRINT CITY.STATE.ZIP$
      LPRINT            'Prints a blank line between labels
      LET LABEL.CTR = LABEL.CTR + 1
WEND
PRINT "End of Job"
END
```

Follow these steps for iteration in which a loop is to be executed a fixed number of times:

1. Initialize a counter before looping.

2. Increment the counter each time you execute the loop.

3. Use the WHILE statement to test the counter. This ensures that the loop is executed the required number of times.

Watch out for a common error made when using a counter: forgetting to initialize the counter at the beginning or to increment it within the loop.

As another example, let us see how you can add five amounts to a total. Suppose you prepare the following program, which contains a logic error:

```
LET TOTAL = 0
LET COUNTER = 0
WHILE COUNTER < 5
    INPUT AMT1
    LET TOTAL = TOTAL + AMT1
WEND
PRINT TOTAL
END
```

The WHILE . . . WEND loop is incorrect because within its sequence of steps there is no instruction to increase or increment the COUNTER. Thus, COUNTER is initialized at 0 and remains at 0 throughout. Since COUNTER will always be less than 5, values for AMT1 are entered and added to TOTAL indefinitely. This error condition is called an infinite loop; that is, the computer will execute the procedure, continually prompting for input, until the programmer or user realizes that there is an error and terminates the program.

The correct coding for the preceding program is:

```
LET TOTAL = 0
LET COUNTER = 0
```

```
WHILE COUNTER < 5
    INPUT AMT1
    LET TOTAL = TOTAL + AMT1
    LET COUNTER = COUNTER + 1 'Counter must be incremented
WEND
PRINT TOTAL
END
```

Once the COUNTER is equal to 5, the WHILE . . . WEND loop will no longer be executed. TOTAL will then print and the run will terminate.

If a program with an infinite loop is run on a mainframe, the computer is normally programmed to automatically terminate a job when it runs too long. On microcomputers using BASIC, you can press the Ctrl key and, while holding it down, press the Break key to exit an infinite loop.

Self-test

How may times will the WHILE . . . WEND be executed in each of the following cases (1 through 4)?

```
1. LET CTR = 5
   LET TOTAL = 0
   WHILE CTR <= 10
       INPUT AMT
       LET TOTAL = TOTAL + AMT
       LET CTR = CTR + 1
   WEND
   PRINT TOTAL

2. LET CTR = 10
   LET TOTAL = 0
   WHILE CTR >= 5
       INPUT AMT
       LET TOTAL = TOTAL + AMT
       LET CTR = CTR - 1
   WEND
   PRINT TOTAL

3. LET CTR = 10
   LET TOTAL = 0
   WHILE CTR >= 10
       INPUT AMT
       LET TOTAL = TOTAL + AMT
   WEND
   PRINT TOTAL
```

```
4. LET CTR = 0
   LET TOTAL = 0
   WHILE CTR <= 5
       LET TOTAL = TOTAL + AMT
       INPUT AMT
       LET CTR = CTR + 1
   WEND
   PRINT TOTAL
```

5. Write a program to calculate and print the sum of even integers from 2 to 2000.

Solutions

1. six times
2. six times
3. infinite loop—CTR is not changed within the loop
4. six times
5.
```
   'This program prints the sum of even numbers from 2-2000
   LET SUM = 0
   LET EVENNO = 2
   WHILE EVENNO <= 2000
       LET SUM = SUM + EVENNO
       LET EVENNO = EVENNO + 2
   WEND
   PRINT "The sum of even numbers from 2-2000 is "; SUM
   END
```

Nested Iterations

All forms of iteration can be **nested**, which means that any one iteration may appear within another. For example, suppose you again wish to prepare mailing labels. This time you want 25 labels for each customer, and the number of customers is variable. In this case, you read one line of input containing (1) customer name, (2) street address, and (3) city state and zip. (Assume that there are no commas between city, state, and zip number.) You print 25 labels for each input line entered. You terminate processing when a customer name is entered as "LAST"; that is, "LAST" is a trailer value indicating that there is no more data. You use an initial input statement and a trailer value here because you do not know how many customers you have.

One method for accomplishing this procedure is to use a WHILE (more data) . . . WEND loop and within that, a WHILE . . . WEND that is executed exactly 25 times. Within the major WHILE . . . WEND loop you establish a counter that begins as zero. Within the minor loop, this counter is increased by 1 each time a label is written. In this way, when the counter is 25, you know you have written 25 labels for each set of input variables. The program for this problem appears in Figure 9.1.

```
'This program prints 25 mailing labels for each customer
INPUT CUSTNAME$, STADDR$, CITYSTATEZIP$
    WHILE CUSTNAME$ <> "LAST"
       LET COUNTER = 0

          WHILE COUNTER < 25
             LPRINT CUSTNAME$
             LPRINT STADDR$
             LPRINT CITYSTATEZIP$
             LPRINT
             LET COUNTER = COUNTER + 1
          WEND

          LPRINT 'Space after each set of labels
          LPRINT 'Space after each set of labels
          INPUT CUSTNAME$, STADDR$, CITYSTATEZIP$
    WEND

    PRINT "End of Job"
    END
```

Figure 9.1
Program showing nested iterations.

This program illustrates the use of nested iteration. The major loop is defined by:

```
WHILE CUSTNAME$ <> "LAST"
   .
   .
   .
WEND      'Outer loop refers to 1st WHILE
```

The loop structure WHILE CUSTNAME$ <> "LAST" to the last WEND is the major iteration. All instructions from WHILE up until the last WEND are part of it. As long as CUSTNAME$ is not equal to "LAST", the entire structure is executed repeatedly. When CUSTNAME$ is finally entered as "LAST", the computer proceeds to the statement following the last WEND, which in this instance prints an end-of-job message. Then, it executes an END, where the program is terminated.

The minor or inner loop is delimited by WHILE COUNTER < 25 on the fifth line to the WEND on the eleventh line. Before the minor iteration or module is executed 25 times, the COUNTER must be set to zero. The computer then executes the minor loop or module 25 times, or until COUNTER = 25. COUNTER is set to 1 after one label is written, to 2 after the second label is written, and so on. This means that when 25 labels have been written, COUNTER will be 25. The minor or inner WHILE . . . WEND will no longer be executed, and control will pass to the next step after the inner loop on the twelfth line. The LPRINTs that follow provide two lines of space between labels, and then the next set of variables is read. This entire process is repeated until a trailer value with a CUSTNAME$ equal to "LAST" is entered, at which point the program ends.

Although setting COUNTER to 0 initially is not required because all numeric variables are automatically set to 0, the outer loop requires this instruction. That is, COUNTER must be set to 0 not only at the beginning, but each time through the major loop. You could, alternatively, initialize COUNTER at 1 instead of 0 and then code WHILE COUNTER <= 25.

The use of a WHILE within a WHILE, as we have just seen, is called a **nested WHILE**. The main (or outer) WHILE usually means that an entire routine or module is to be executed for as long as there is input. This routine or module may itself have some iteration or sequence of steps to be repeated that calls for another WHILE. Keep in mind that the *last* (or outer) WEND statement refers to the *first* WHILE, and inner WEND statements refer to inner WHILEs. We recommend that you indent instructions within loops for clarity, as shown in Figure 9.2. When writing a program, remember that each WHILE is matched to the closest WEND.

FOR . . . NEXT Statements

A loop is a form of iteration in which a sequence of instructions is executed repeatedly. We have used several types of loops for iteration. FOR . . . NEXT statements can perform many loop control functions automatically. In this section we consider the FOR . . . NEXT for looping.

FOR . . . NEXT as Another Iterative Technique Suppose you want to compute the amount of money you will accumulate at the end of one, two, and three years if you deposit a specified amount at a given interest rate. Assume that the interest is compounded annually, which means that in year 2, the new principal will be the original principal plus the interest from year 1 and that the rate of return is based on this increased value for the principal.

The new principal for each of the three years is:

New Principal after year 1 = Original Principal $(1 + \text{Rate})$
New Principal after year 2 = Original Principal $(1 + \text{Rate})^2$
New Principal after year 3 = Original Principal $(1 + \text{Rate})^3$

The general formula for computing compound interest is:

$$P_n = P_o (1 + r)^n$$

where: P_o = original principal
         P_n = principal after n years
         r = interest rate
         n = number of years

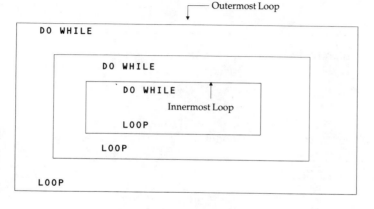

Figure 9.2
Indented inner loops within outer loops:

When n is 1, P_n is equal to the total amount of money after one year of investment of an initial amount (P_o) at a given rate of interest (r). When n is 2, P_n is equal to the total amount after two years of investment. When n is 3, P_n is equal to the total amount after three years of investment.

Let us begin with an illustration that focuses on compound interest for this three-year period. The input to be entered consists of a principal amount (P_o) and interest rate (r). The number of years to be invested (n) will be predefined as 3.

The output will consist of a chart indicating the value of the principal plus interest for each of three years of investment. The following provides an example of the displayed input and output:

```
ENTER PRINCIPAL AMOUNT:
?    2000
ENTER INTEREST RATE: (e.g., 8% AS 8.0):
?    10.0
INVESTMENT CHART FOR 2000 AT 10% INTEREST
    YEAR        AMOUNT
    1           2200
    2           2420
    3           2662
```

We will now write a program that computes the total, where values of P (principal) and r (rate of interest) are to be entered as input. We are interested in the results when n equals 1, 2, and 3. The following method does not use any loops:

```
PRINT "Enter Principal Amount:"
INPUT PRINCIPAL
PRINT "Enter Interest Rate (e.g., 8% as 8.0):"
INPUT RATE
PRINT
PRINT "INVESTMENT CHART FOR "; Principal; " AT "; RATE; "% INTEREST"
PRINT "    YEAR        AMOUNT"
LET RATE = RATE / 100

┌─────────────────────────────────────────────────────────┐
│ LET AMOUNT1 = PRINCIPAL * (1 + RATE) ^ 1                  │
│ PRINT "    1        "; AMOUNT1                            │
│ LET AMOUNT2 = PRINCIPAL * (1 + RATE) ^ 2                  │
│ PRINT "    2        "; AMOUNT2                            │
│ LET AMOUNT3 = PRINCIPAL * (1 + RATE) ^ 3                  │
│ PRINT "    3        "; AMOUNT3                            │
└─────────────────────────────────────────────────────────┘

END
```

The screen display would be:

```
Enter Principal Amount:
?100
Enter Interest Rate (e.g., 8% as 8.0):
?5.0
```

This is followed by:

```
INVESTMENT CHART FOR 100 AT 5.0% INTEREST
    YEAR        AMOUNT
     1          105
     2          110.25
     3          115.7625
```

To represent all values as dollars-and-cents figures use a PRINT USING as follows:

```
PRINT "    1    "; ' ; means line is not terminated
PRINT USING "###.##"; AMOUNT1
```

These lines would replace PRINT "   1   "; AMOUNT1 in the program.

Notice that the boxed entries within the program have several lines that are similar; that is, the arithmetic operations use the same basic formula. For year 1, $(1 + RATE)$ is multiplied by PRINCIPAL. For year 2, $(1 + RATE)^2$, or $(1 + RATE) \times (1 + RATE)$, is multiplied by PRINCIPAL. For year 3, $(1 + RATE)^3$, or $(1 + RATE) \times (1 + RATE) \times (1 + RATE)$, is multiplied by PRINCIPAL. Any sequence of steps that is repeated with an incremented set of values is best coded with a loop that executes a single sequence repeatedly.

In this program, one routine could be coded to compute the three values. This one routine could use a variable exponent called NO.OF.YEARS, for example, which begins as 1 and is incremented by 1 each time the routine is executed until the variable exceeds 3. In other words, a loop can be established to be executed three times, varying NO.OF.YEARS from 1 to 3.

The next method uses a WHILE . . . WEND structure:

```
PRINT "Enter Principal Amount:"
INPUT PRINCIPAL
PRINT "Enter Interest Rate (e.g., 8% as 8.0):"
INPUT RATE
PRINT
PRINT "INVESTMENT CHART FOR "; PRINCIPAL; " AT "; RATE; "% INTEREST"
PRINT "    YEAR        AMOUNT"
```

```
LET RATE = RATE / 100
LET NO.OF.YEARS = 1
WHILE NO.OF.YEARS <= 3
    LET AMOUNT = PRINCIPAL * (1 + RATE) ^ NO.OF.YEARS
    PRINT "    "; NO.OF.YEARS; "      "; AMOUNT
    LET NO.OF.YEARS = NO.OF.YEARS + 1
WEND
END
```

Notice that this program uses a WHILE . . . WEND loop. The sequence of instructions to be repeated is within the WHILE routine. Since NO.OF.YEARS is not greater than 3, the statements within the WHILE . . . WEND loop are executed for the first time with NO.OF.YEARS = 1. Then 1 is added to NO.OF.YEARS and the computer tests again to see if NO.OF.YEARS is greater than 3. Since it is now 2, which is not greater than 3, the statements within the WHILE . . . WEND loop are executed again with NO.OF.YEARS = 2. Then with NO.OF.YEARS = 3, the WHILE . . . WEND loop is executed again. After the third time through this loop, 1 is added to NO.OF.YEARS, which makes it 4. Since 4 is greater than 3, the loop is not performed again and the program ends.

The previous solution shows that you can perform a series of operations by using a variable NO.OF.YEARS that begins as 1 and is incremented until it reaches 3. The FOR . . . NEXT statement is typically used to perform a loop a predefined number of times in which a variable needs to be incremented, as in this case.

The FOR . . . NEXT structure performs several functions. It establishes a variable, increments the variable, and specifies the range in which the variable is to vary. For our problem, we have:

```
FOR NO.OF.YEARS = 1 TO 3
    LET AMOUNT = PRINCIPAL * (1 + RATE) ^ NO.OF.YEARS
    PRINT AMOUNT
NEXT NO.OF.YEARS
```

The statements within the FOR . . . NEXT structure will be executed for the first time with the variable NO.OF.YEARS equal to 1. The instruction FOR NO.OF.YEARS = 1 TO 3 means that the computer will repeat the steps within the FOR . . . NEXT structure first with NO.OF.YEARS = 2 and then NO.OF.YEARS = 3.

Thus, the procedure is executed three times, first with NO.OF.YEARS = 1, then NO.OF.YEARS = 2, and finally NO.OF.YEARS = 3. Now the program will continue with the statement after the NEXT, which in this case is the end of the program. With the FOR . . . NEXT loop there is no need to initialize the counter (NO.OF.YEARS here) to 1 or to increment it by 1 each time through the loop. This is handled by the FOR . . . NEXT structure itself.

The full program using the FOR . . . NEXT loop follows:

```
PRINT "Enter Principal Amount:"
INPUT PRINCIPAL
```

```
PRINT "Enter Interest Rate (e.g., 8% as 8.0):"
INPUT RATE
PRINT
PRINT "INVESTMENT CHART FOR "; PRINCIPAL; " AT "; RATE; "% INTEREST"
PRINT "    YEAR      AMOUNT"
LET RATE = RATE / 100
FOR NO.OF.YEARS = 1 to 3
    LET AMOUNT = PRINCIPAL * (1 + RATE) ^ NO.OF.YEARS
    PRINT "    "; NO.OF.YEARS; "       "; AMOUNT
NEXT NO.OF.YEARS
END
```

The output will be the same regardless of which method you use for coding the program. The initial screen display will be:

```
Enter Principal Amount:
?100
Enter Interest Rate (e.g., 8% as 8.0):
?5.0
```

This is followed by:

```
INVESTMENT CHART FOR 100 AT 5.0% INTEREST
    YEAR        AMOUNT
     1          105
     2          110.25
     3          115.7625
```

Use the FOR . . . NEXT whenever a sequence is to be repeated a fixed number of times and a variable needs to be incremented each time through the sequence. Remember to use a PRINT USING to display the amounts as dollars-and-cents values.

Refinements of the FOR . . . NEXT Thus far we have used numeric literals in FOR . . . NEXT loops for the starting and ending points of the variable NO.OF.YEARS (such as FOR NO.OF.YEARS = 1 TO 3). The starting and ending points, or delimiters, of the FOR . . . NEXT could also be numeric variables. Moreover, the starting delimiter need not be 1. Consider the following two examples:

Example 1

```
LET S = 1
FOR N = S TO 10        'N will vary from 1 to 10
    .
    .
    .
NEXT N
```

Example 2

```
LET T = 5
FOR N = 1 TO T        'N will vary from 1 to 5
  .
  .
  .
NEXT N
```

Keep in mind that if the beginning delimiter is greater than the ending delimiter in a FOR . . . NEXT, the loop is not executed at all. In the following example, the FOR . . . NEXT does not get executed:

```
LET I = 10
LET J = 5
FOR N = I TO J
   .
   .
   .
NEXT N
```

Also, you can increment the variable in a FOR . . . NEXT by a value other than 1. Consider first the following example in which I is incremented by 1 each time through the loop:

```
    FOR I = 1 TO 5
      .
      .
      .
    NEXT I
```

The computer executes the loop five times. The first time I has a value of 1, then 2, until it reaches 5. When I is 5, the loop is executed a fifth time, and then the statement following the NEXT is executed. Thus I is incremented by 1 each time the loop is executed. Using a STEP clause, however, you can increment I by any value you wish.

Suppose you want to sum the odd numbers from 1 to 101, inclusive of the endpoints, using a FOR . . . NEXT loop. You could code the following:

```
LET T = 0
```

```
FOR I = 1 TO 101 STEP 2
    LET T = T + I
NEXT I
```

```
PRINT "The Sum of Odd Numbers from 1-101 is "; T
```

In this FOR . . . NEXT loop, I, the integer, is initially set equal to 1. T is incremented by the value of I, and then I is incremented by 2. I continues to be incremented by 2 until it equals 101 and the FOR . . . NEXT loop is terminated.

The STEP clause could specify a variable instead of a value. Thus the preceding example could be written as:

```
LET S = 2
FOR I = 1 TO 101 STEP S
    LET T = T + I
NEXT I
```

Moreover, the STEP clause can be used to decrease the values in the variable. The following example is also correct:

```
FOR I = 101 TO 1 STEP -2
    LET T = T + I
NEXT I
```

If the STEP clause is omitted, the default STEP value is 1. This means that the computer assumes you want to increment the variable by 1 each time. Thus, the following two instructions produce identical results:

```
FOR I = 1 TO 5    and    FOR I = 1 TO 5 STEP 1
```

Do not change the variable used with a FOR . . . NEXT loop within the loop itself. The following type of coding could produce errors:

• **INVALID**

```
FOR I = 1 TO 5
    .
    .
    .
    LET I = . . .
NEXT I
```

I is the variable in this FOR . . . NEXT. It should not be altered within the loop by the programmer as it was in the preceding example.

Do not use the variable defined by a FOR . . . NEXT outside the loop. Consider the following invalid coding:

• **INVALID**

```
FOR I = 1 TO 5
    .
    .
    .
```

```
NEXT I
PRINT I    'I should not be accessed outside the loop
```

As I varies from 1 to 5 in the FOR . . . NEXT, you might assume that 5 or 6 will print when the preceding instructions are executed. In fact, I has predictable values only within the FOR . . . NEXT and should not be accessed outside the loop.

FOR . . . NEXT loops, like all other iterative structures, can be nested, which means that you may include FOR . . . NEXTs within FOR . . . NEXTs. When nesting FOR . . . NEXT loops, be sure to keep in mind the fact that each NEXT is matched to the closest FOR. Consider the following invalid coding:

• **INVALID**

```
FOR N = 1 TO 5
    .
    .
    .
FOR M = 1 TO 10
    .
    .
    .
NEXT N
    .
    .
    .
NEXT M
```

The NEXT N and NEXT M instructions must be reversed to make this structure work properly. That is, the initial FOR N = 1 TO 5 is the major loop and must be linked to the outermost NEXT N. The minor, or second, FOR M = 1 TO 10 should be linked to the first, or inner, NEXT M. If the minor FOR . . . NEXT loop were indented in the preceding code, it would have been easier to detect the error.

As a coding guideline, indent a FOR . . . NEXT within a FOR . . . NEXT loop, and indent all statements within the minor loop as well. Your programs will be easier to read and debug. Press the Tab key once to indent eight spaces on a line; press it again to indent another eight spaces.

Which Iterative Technique to Use

An iterative structure can be coded using either a WHILE . . . WEND or a FOR . . . NEXT structure. Most programmers prefer to use a WHILE . . . WEND loop when the number of iterations is unknown or varies each time the program is to be run. In other words, if the number of iterations depends on the input, it is best to use a WHILE . . . WEND structure. If, however, the number of times an iteration is to be executed is fixed, it is best to use a FOR . . . NEXT loop.

Self-test

1. What is wrong with the following program excerpt?

```
FOR N = 1 TO 4
    INPUT AMT
    PRINT AMT
NEXT I
```

2. Print a multiplication table as follows using FOR ... NEXT looping:

1	2	3	4	5
2	4	6	8	10
3	6	9	12	15
4	8	12	16	20
5	10	15	20	25

3. Code question 2 using a WHILE ... WEND loop.
4. Using a FOR ... NEXT, write a program to calculate and print the sum of even numbers from 2 to 2000 inclusive of the endpoints.
5. Calculate N factorial (N!) where N is an input variable. N factorial = N $\times$ (N $-$ 1) $\times$ ... 1 (for example, 5! = 5 $\times$ 4 $\times$ 3 $\times$ 2 $\times$ 1 = 120).

Solutions

1. The NEXT statement should be NEXT N.
2. Program:

```
FOR N = 1 TO 5
    LPRINT N, N * 2, N * 3, N * 4, N * 5
    LPRINT
NEXT N
END
```

Displayed output:

1	2	3	4	5
2	4	6	8	10
3	6	9	12	15
4	8	12	16	20
5	10	15	20	25

3. WHILE ... WEND loop:

```
N = 1
WHILE N <= 5
    LPRINT N, N * 2, N * 3, N * 4, N * 5
```

```
            LPRINT
            N = N + 1
        WEND
        END
```

4. FOR . . . NEXT loop:

```
        TOTAL = 0
        FOR NUMBER = 2 TO 2000 STEP 2
            TOTAL = TOTAL + NUMBER
        NEXT NUMBER
        PRINT TOTAL
        END
```

5. N Factorial (N!):

```
        TOTAL = 1
        INPUT N
        FOR CTR = N TO 1 STEP -1
            TOTAL = TOTAL * CTR
        NEXT CTR
        PRINT N; "FACTORIAL = "; TOTAL
        END
```

Introduction to Subroutines for Top-Down Modular Programming

Thus far in this text, we have focused on QBASIC and BASICA syntax and three of the four logical control constructs necessary for writing well-designed programs. You have learned how to use pseudocode to map out the logic in your programs before you begin coding. Moreover, you have been introduced to the concept of top-down programming.

In this section we consider top-down modular programming in detail. Top-down modular programs are easy to code, debug, maintain, and modify. Recall that a module is routine, or a group of instructions that function as a unit and that perform a specific set of operations.

Subroutines Defined

One method for writing a modular top-down BASIC program is with the use of subroutines. Recall that a subroutine is another term for a module:

Subroutines can minimize duplication of effort. Consider the following program excerpt.

```
PRINT "Enter Customer No:"
INPUT CUSTNO
PRINT "Enter Part Description:"
INPUT PARTDESCRIPTION$
PRINT "Enter Unit Price:"
INPUT UNITPRICE
PRINT "Enter Qty Ordered:"
INPUT QTYORDERED
```

```
WHILE CUSTNO < 999
      LET BALDUE = UNITPRICE * QTYORDERED
      LPRINT "Customer "; CUSTNO; "Owes: "
      LPRINT BALDUE; "For Part "; PARTDESCRIPTION$
```

```
PRINT "Enter Customer No:"
INPUT CUSTNO
PRINT "Enter Part Description:"
INPUT PARTDESCRIPTION$
PRINT "Enter Unit Price:"
INPUT UNITPRICE
PRINT "Enter Qty Ordered:"
INPUT QTYORDERED
```

```
WEND
LPRINT "End of Report"
END
```

Each of the boxed entries represents a module—a subroutine or sequence of steps that accomplishes a given function; in this case, the module prompts for input and enters the input as well.

Note that both boxed entries are the same. They appear in two places—as part of an initial read routine and then, again, at the end of the WHILE . . . WEND loop. Repeating the boxed set of instructions twice is not only cumbersome but it increases the risk of errors. Instead, a subroutine can be written as a separate series of statements (a module) and can then be executed in the program whenever it is needed.

A GOSUB is a statement that causes execution of a separate subroutine. After the computer executes the subroutine, it returns control to the statement following the GOSUB.

BASICA GOSUB line # in BASICA is the instruction that causes execution of the statements at the subroutine specified by the label. You could write, therefore:

```
10        GOSUB 1000
```

```
20      WHILE CUSTNO < 999
30          LET BALDUE = UNITPRICE * QTYORDERED
40          LPRINT "Customer "; CUSTNO; "Owes: "
50          LPRINT BALDUE ; "For Part "; PARTDESCRIPTION$

60          GOSUB 1000

70      WEND
80      LPRINT "End of Report"
90      END
```

GOSUB 1000 instructs the computer to execute a module located at line 1000. The module itself will follow the END statement. The GOSUB causes execution of all of the instructions within that module; it must end with a RETURN statement. After all of the instructions within the subroutine are executed, control returns to the statement in the main program following the GOSUB. The return point will be line 20 after the first execution of the GOSUB, and it will be line 70 after every other execution of the GOSUB.

The subroutine that begins at line 1000 is itself coded after the END and must have a RETURN as a scope terminator:

```
10   GOSUB
     .
     .
     .
100  END
1000 '*******************************************
1010 ' This subroutine prompts for & gets input
1020 '*******************************************

1030     PRINT "Enter Customer No:"
1040     INPUT CustNo
1050     PRINT "Enter Part Description:"
1060     INPUT PartDescription$
1070     PRINT "Enter Unit Price:"
1080     INPUT UnitPrice
1090     PRINT "Enter Qty Ordered:"
1100     INPUT QtyOrdered

1110 RETURN
```

Note that the subroutine at line number 1000 is executed twice from the main program. The actual sequence of steps in the subroutine is, however, coded only once at the end of the program. Any number of subroutines may be included after the END statement.

A sequence of instructions that appears more than once in a program can be coded as a separate subroutine and can be executed from the main program with a GOSUB instruction, as we just showed. Even sequences that appear only once are often best coded as a subroutine, if they represent a cohesive entity. This is especially true in IF statements where you are restricted to three lines of coding. For example:

- **BASICA**

```
10 IF AMT1 = AMT2 THEN . . .   ← Sequence of steps to be executed
                                  if AMT1 and AMT2 are equal

   ELSE . . .   ← Sequence of steps to be executed
                   if AMT1 and AMT2 are unequal
```

Each sequence is a cohesive set of instructions that is collectively executed under certain conditions. The preferred form for this IF statement is:

- **BASICA**

```
10 IF  AMT1 = AMT2 THEN
       GOSUB 1000      'This will process data if AMT1 = AMT2
   ELSE GOSUB 2000     'This will process data if AMT1 <> AMT2
```

In this way, each GOSUB can have separate instructions on separate lines without the need for using colons to separate instructions in an IF statement and without having to worry about exceeding 255 characters in the entire IF statement.

QBASIC In QBASIC, subroutines are defined by name, not line numbers:

```
IF  AMT1 = AMT2 THEN
    GOSUB EQUALROUTINE
ELSE
    GOSUB UNEQUALROUTINE
END IF
  .
  .
  .
END

┌─────────────────────────────┐
│ EQUALROUTINE:               │
│   .                         │
│   .                         │
│   .                         │
│ RETURN                      │
└─────────────────────────────┘
```

```
UNEQUALROUTINE:
        .
        .
        .
RETURN
```

Using Subroutines in Top-Down Modular Programming

When planning a program like the one we just presented, it would be unwise to begin by focusing on the syntax in the subroutines. Instead, it is best to develop the logic by focusing on the structure of the program first; leave the details in a subroutine for later.

Thus, when coding a program, you may include a GOSUB in the main program to designate any subroutine or sequence of instructions that you wish to code in detail later. This technique is called top-down modular programming. Long and complex programs could contain many GOSUBs, which keeps the main module clear and free from details; the details are left for the subroutines, which are coded last.

We encourage you to code top-down programs in this way. That is, code any sequence of steps that represents a related set of operations, such as printing headings or entering a series of variables, as a module or subroutine. The purpose of this top-down modular approach is to allow you to focus on the structure rather than the syntax in the main body of the program. Similarly, any series of steps that is executed from more than one place in a program should be coded in a subroutine and executed from the main program with a GOSUB. Consider the following examples:

- **QBASIC**

```
'This program prints amounts - 25 per page
GOSUB PRINTHEADINGS
INPUT AMT1
WHILE AMT1 < 999
    LPRINT "Amount = "; AMT1
    LINECTR = LINECTR + 1
    'LineCtr keeps track of the number of lines printed
    IF  LINECTR = 25 THEN
        GOSUB 1000           'We want 25 lines per page
    END IF                   'Used with QBASIC only
    INPUT AMT1
WEND
END
'*****************************************************
' This subroutine prints headings
'*****************************************************
```

```
PRINTHEADINGS:
     LPRINT "          DETAIL  REPORT  "
     LINECTR = 0                'Reinitializes Line Counter
RETURN
```

- **BASICA**

```
10 'This program prints amounts - 25 per page
20 GOSUB 1000
30 INPUT AMT1
40 WHILE AMT1 < 999
50     LPRINT "Amount = "; AMT1
60     LINECTR = LINECTR + 1
70     'LineCtr keeps track of the number of lines printed
80     IF  LINECTR = 25 THEN
            GOSUB 1000              'We want 25 lines per page
90     INPUT AMT1
100 WEND
110 END
1000 '********************************************************
1010 ' This subroutine prints headings
1020 '********************************************************
1030          LPRINT "          DETAIL  REPORT  "
1040          LINECTR = 0                'Reinitializes Line Counter
1050 RETURN
```

The subroutine, at PRINTHEADINGS for QBASIC and at line 1000 for BASICA, that prints the headings is performed at the beginning of the program and then, again, whenever LINECTR = 25. After the RETURN is executed, control returns to the statement following the GOSUB instruction. Initially, after the PRINTHEAD-INGS module (beginning at line 1000 in BASICA) is executed, control returns to the first INPUT statement (line 30 in BASICA). If a GOSUB is executed from within the loop, then control returns to the INPUT AMT1 statement.

Line number 1000 in BASICA was used for our subroutine just because it is a round number; any line number after 110 (the END statement) could have been used. The END statement is necessary here to separate the main body of the program from its subroutines.

All logical control constructs, including GOSUBS, can be nested. This means any such construct can include the same construct within it. A GOSUB, for example, can be written in a module that is itself executed by a GOSUB.

Subroutines can appear in any order as long as they follow the END statement. We recommend, however, that you code major subroutines before minor ones so that your programs will be top-down.

Common GOSUB Errors

There are two common causes of GOSUB errors:

1. Failure to include a RETURN with a GOSUB results in a logic error.

2. Failure to include an END statement in its proper place causes an error. Be sure that the END statement precedes the first subroutine in the program; omitting this will result in a logic error.

ON . . . GOSUB for the Case Structure

We have learned that there are four logical control constructs: sequence, IF-THEN-ELSE, iteration, and CASE. The Case structure, which consists of selecting a module from a series of items or menu, is coded using ON . . . GOSUB.

Consider the following menu that may appear on a screen:

```
                        Payroll Procedure Menu



        Salary Change         ┌───┐
                              │ 1 │
                              └───┘

        Name Change           ┌───┐
                              │ 2 │
                              └───┘

        Address Change        ┌───┐
                              │ 3 │
                              └───┘

        Department Change     ┌───┐
                              │ 4 │
                              └───┘

        Type a Number 1-4     ┌───┐
                              │   │
                              └───┘
```

The user inputs a number from 1 to 4; different procedures will be executed, depending on which number is entered. Although you could use simple IF statements to test the value entered, a CASE construct is clearer and more efficient. Here is the pseudocode for this structure:

```
CASE MenuItem
      WHEN 1 Process Salary Change
      WHEN 2 Process Name Change
      WHEN 3 Process Address Change
      WHEN 4 Process Department Change
END CASE
```

This structure can be coded in QBASIC or BASICA with an ON . . . GOSUB (some versions of BASIC like QBASIC have additional CASE structures—see Appendix B).

- **BASICA**

```
10   '*********************************************
20   'An Example of a Case Structure
30   ' The program begins with a main module first
40   '*********************************************
```

```
  50   INPUT MENU.ITEM
  60   ON MENU.ITEM GOSUB 1000, 2000, 3000, 4000
   .      .
   .      .
   .      .
 999   END
1000   '*****************************************
1010   ' This subprogram defines the Salary
1020   ' Change Procedure
1030   '*****************************************
   .      .
   .      .
   .      .
1999   RETURN ' This instruction returns you to main module
2000   '*****************************************
2010   ' This subprogram defines the Name
2030   ' Change Procedure
2040   '*****************************************
   .      .
   .      .
   .      .
2999   RETURN ' This instruction returns you to main module
3000   '*****************************************
3010   ' This subprogram defines the Address
3020   ' Change Procedure
3030   '*****************************************
   .      .
   .      .
   .      .
3999   RETURN ' This instruction returns you to main module
4000   '*****************************************
4010   ' This subprogram defines the Department
4020   ' Change Procedure
4030   '*****************************************
   .      .
   .      .
   .      .
4999   RETURN ' This instruction returns you to main module
```

Each of the separate subroutines is a module that is executed if the specified condition is met. That is, if MENU.ITEM = 1, the first line number specified in the ON . . . GOSUB is executed; thus, module 1000, which handles a Salary Change Procedure, would be executed. If MENU.ITEM is a 2, the second line number in the ON . . . GOSUB would be executed; that is, module 2000, which handles a Name Change Procedure would be executed, and so on.

ADVANTAGES OF USING GOSUBS
IN TOP-DOWN MODULAR PROGRAMS

- Programs are easier to read and maintain.

- Duplicate coding is avoided.

- The logic in the program is easier to follow.

- The structure of the program is easier to design.

GUIDELINES FOR CODING SUBROUTINES

- Make each subroutine a self-contained unit representing a single type of operation or function.

- Give each subroutine a single purpose. (For example, use two separate subroutines to perform two separate tasks.)

- Keep subroutines short.

- Code subroutines in a top-down (hierarchical) manner.

Self-test

Consider the following subroutine:

- QBASIC

```
SUB1:
    SUM = SUM + EVENNUM
    EVENNUM = EVENNUM + 2
RETURN
```

- BASICA

```
1000   'SUBROUTINE 1
1010      SUM = SUM + EVENNUM
1020      EVENNUM = EVENNUM + 2
1030   RETURN
```

1. Write a program that calls the above subroutine to calculate the sum of even numbers from 2 to 2000, including the endpoints.
2. Write a program that calls the above subroutine to calculate the sum of even numbers from 50 to 3002, including the endpoints.
3. Write a program that calls a subroutine to calculate the sum of integers from 1 to 2500, excluding the endpoints. Then code the subroutine.

4. Write a program that calls a subroutine to calculate N! (referred to as N factorial) where N! = (N) × (N − 1) × (N − 2) × ... × 1 (for example, 5! = 5 × 4 × 3 × 2 × 1 = 120). Then code the subroutine.
5. (T or F) There must be an END statement before a subroutine can be coded.

Solutions

1. QBASIC program:

```
SUM = 0
EVENNUM = 2
WHILE EVENNUM <= 2000
    GOSUB SUB1                'Use line numbers in BASICA
WEND
PRINT SUM
END
```

2. QBASIC program:

```
SUM = 0
EVENNUM = 50
WHILE EVENNUM <= 3002
    GOSUB SUB1                'Use line numbers in BASICA
WEND
PRINT SUM
END
```

3. BASICA program:

```
10   SUM = 0
20   NUMBER = 1
30   WHILE NUMBER < 2499
40        GOSUB 1000          'Use subroutine name in QBASIC
50   WEND
60   PRINT SUM
70   END
1000 'Add numbers               {Subroutine name goes here in QBASIC
1010      NUMBER = NUMBER + 1
1020      SUM = SUM + NUMBER
1030 RETURN
```

4. BASICA program:

```
10   RESULT = 1
20   INPUT NUMBER
30   FOR FACTOR = NUMBER TO 1 STEP -1
```

```
40       GOSUB 1000              'Use subroutine name in QBASIC
50   NEXT FACTOR
60   PRINT NUMBER; "Factorial = "; RESULT
70   END
1000 'Calculates Factorial      {Subroutine name goes here in QBASIC
1010     RESULT = RESULT * FACTOR
1020 RETURN
```

5. T

10

Array Processing

Introduction to Arrays

Arrays are used in programming to process a series of variables. These variables may be either all numeric or all string. The major uses of arrays include:

- Storing a series of data elements each of the same type (for example, all numeric or all string variables).

- Storing a series of totals to which input amounts are added; after all data is accumulated, the totals can be printed.

- Storing a table to be used for "looking up" values.

Using an Array to Store a Series of Data Elements

Suppose you want to read in and process 20 exam grades, one for each student in a class. Using traditional methods, you would need to input 20 separate variables, one for each exam:

```
INPUT EXAM1
INPUT EXAM2
    .
    .
    .
INPUT EXAM20
```

Moreover, obtaining an average of the 20 exams would require a great deal of tedious coding:

```
AVERAGE = (EXAM1 + EXAM2 + . . . EXAM20) / 20
```

The dots or ellipses (. . .) mean that the programmer would have to specifically list all 20 variables to be used in calculating the average.

All 20 exams are numeric variables that can be defined with a single name referred to as an **array**.

Using the DIM Statement to Define the Size of the Array

The name and size of an array may be defined with a DIMension or DIM statement. To store 20 exam values in an array where you access the first as EXAM(1), the second as EXAM(2), and so on, you could establish the array as follows:

```
DIM EXAM(20)
```

The following is an example of how the EXAM array would appear in storage:

DIM EXAM(20)

0th EXAM	1st EXAM	2nd EXAM	. . .	20th EXAM
(Unused)	Exam (1)	Exam (2)	. . .	Exam (20)

EXAM is called an array, and each variable is an element in that array. There are actually 21 elements in an array set up as DIM EXAM(20). They are EXAM(0) (not used), EXAM(1), EXAM(2), . . . EXAM(20). The 0th is not used, and the first through the twentieth are referred to as EXAM(1) through EXAM(20), respectively.

All elements in an array must be of the same type. In this instance, each element is a numeric variable. As noted, if you establish an array as DIM EXAM(20), EXAM(1) refers to the first exam that you will reference, and EXAM(20) refers to the last EXAM you will reference. To avoid confusion, we do not use the 0th element at all.

The DIM statement that defines an array should precede all instructions that process the array. Thus the following sequence is *incorrect*:

- **INVALID**

```
LET EXAM(20) = 0
    .
    .
    .
DIM EXAM(20)   'DIM must precede the assignment above
```

A DIM statement is not required for all arrays. If you do not include a DIM statement but use an array in your processing, BASIC assumes that the array has a maximum of 11 elements. In this example it also assumes that the elements are numbered EXAM(0) through EXAM(10).

```
INPUT EXAM(0)     'This is the first element of the array
INPUT EXAM(1)     'This is the second element of the array
```

```
     •     '11 is the maximum array
     •     'size unless you use a DIM
INPUT EXAM(10)
```

In our example, if a DIM statement does not precede the INPUT instructions, the default is DIM EXAM(10), which has elements numbered EXAM(0) . . . EXAM(10). No error message occurs when referencing an EXAM as long as you do not reference any element outside that range (0–10). Therefore, to code INPUT EXAM(11) without a preceding DIM statement would cause a syntax error.

CODING GUIDELINES

To ensure proper handling and to make your programs clearer, always use DIM statements when processing an array. In the statement DIM array(m), 0 is the lowest element number in the array and m is the highest element number in the array.

Accessing an Array Element Using a Subscript

Let us consider the EXAM array established with DIM EXAM(20), and let us assume that you have already entered input into EXAM(1) through EXAM(20). Remember that EXAM(0) is not used. To access any one of the 20 exams, use the array name, EXAM, along with the entry within parentheses, which we call a **subscript**. The subscript indicates which of the 20 entries (1 through 20, respectively) you want to access. (Although a subscript of 0 refers to a valid array element, we are not using this element here.) For example, you would access the first student's grade as EXAM(1), the second student's grade as EXAM(2), and so on. If the 20 exams were already entered and stored in the computer, you could print the fifth student's grade by coding:

```
50 PRINT "GRADE FOR STUDENT 5 IS  "; EXAM(5)
```

The subscript, then, specifies the particular element in the array that you want to access. In our example, the subscript is the number of the actual element you want. The subscripts vary from 1 to m, where m is the number of array elements.

A subscript along with the array name refers to any element within the array. In our example, if DIM EXAM(20) is coded, the subscript for EXAM can have a value from 1 through 20. Any other value (except 0), such as the two that follow, would result in an error.

```
PRINT EXAM(.5)
PRINT EXAM(21)
```

Subscripts: Integers, Variables, or Arithmetic Expressions

Thus far we have focused on subscripts that are integers. A subscript, however, may also be a variable that contains an integer. Suppose you define a numeric variable along with the EXAM array as follows.

```
DIM EXAM(20)
LET I = 1
```

You could print the first exam grade with either of the following coding:

```
PRINT EXAM(I)
```

or

```
PRINT EXAM(1)
```

Subscripts, then, identify specific items in an array, and they can be either integers or variables that contain integers. Using a variable rather than a fixed integer as a subscript enables you to vary the content of the subscript so that you can process a series of items within a single procedure. Suppose you want to find the average of the 20 exams that have been stored in an array. You can use integers as subscripts, but to do so does not reduce the coding at all.

```
AVERAGE = (EXAM(1) + EXAM(2) + . . . EXAM(20)) / 20
```

It is far more efficient to write a loop that adds one exam at a time to a total where the exam is referenced by a variable subscript. You can vary the content of the subscript from 1 to 20 so that all 20 exams are added to the total.

Using FOR . . . NEXT for Processing an Array

Assume that all 20 exams are already stored in the EXAM array. The procedure for calculating an average can be coded with a FOR . . . NEXT loop as follows:

```
'Calculate an Average assuming Exam1-Exam20
'Have already been entered
DIM EXAM(20)
TOTAL = 0
FOR I = 1 TO 20
    TOTAL = TOTAL + EXAM(I)
NEXT I
AVERAGE = TOTAL / 20
PRINT "Average = "; AVERAGE
END
```

We used a FOR . . . NEXT for initializing and incrementing subscripts until the entire array was processed. We could have used a WHILE . . . WEND loop as well, but we would then need to initialize and increment the subscript with additional instructions. The FOR . . . NEXT loop does this automatically.

CODING GUIDELINE

Any iterative structure (FOR . . . NEXT or WHILE . . . WEND) can be used to process elements in an array. We recommend using the FOR . . . NEXT statement when processing all array elements because the subscript or index variable is automatically initialized and incremented properly. This results in shorter, clearer code.

Let us consider additional examples of procedures that process an array. For example, to find the highest exam grade in the class, we can code the following procedure:

```
'Find highest grade
'Assume array already entered
DIM EXAM(20)
HIGHEST = 0          'Initialize Highest
FOR I = 1 TO 20
    IF  EXAM(I) > HIGHEST THEN     'Press Ctrl+End for BASICA
        HIGHEST = EXAM(I)
    END IF             'Used with QBASIC
NEXT I
PRINT "Highest Grade is "; HIGHEST
```

To print the number of the student who has the highest score, you need to save the subscript number of the grade in HIGHEST as well as the grade itself:

```
'Find Student with the highest grade
'Assume array already entered
DIM EXAM(20)
HIGHEST = 0
FOR I = 1 TO 20
    IF  EXAM(I) > HIGHEST THEN     'Press Ctrl+End for BASICA
        HIGHEST = EXAM(I) : STUDENT = I
    END IF             'Used with QBASIC
NEXT I
PRINT "Student "; STUDENT; "Has Highest Grade "
```

To find the number of students who received a grade of 80 or more, you would write this code:

```
'Find the number of students
'With a grade of 80 or more
'Assume array already entered
```

```
DIM EXAM(20)
COUNT = 0
FOR I = 1 TO 20
    IF  EXAM(I) >= 80 THEN          'Press Ctrl+End for BASICA
        COUNT = COUNT + 1
    END IF            'Used with QBASIC
NEXT I
PRINT  "No. of Students with a Grade of 80 or More is "; COUNT
```

Reading Data into an Array

Thus far we have assumed that data has already been read and stored in our EXAM array. Let us now consider the routine to input the 20 exams.

```
'Input data to an array
DIM EXAM(20)
FOR I = 1 TO 20
    PRINT "Enter Exam Score "; I
    INPUT EXAM(I)
NEXT I
```

Note that the array need not be initialized to 0, since data will be read into it.

Let us look at another example. The following will load into an array seven daily sales totals:

```
DIM SALES(7)
FOR I = 1 TO 7
    PRINT "Enter Sales Total for "; I
    INPUT SALES(I)
NEXT I
```

Assuming that the array is loaded, calculate the weekly total as follows:

```
TOTAL = 0
FOR I = 1 TO 7
    TOTAL = TOTAL + SALES(I)
NEXT I
PRINT "The Total Sales is "; TOTAL
```

Now assuming that the array is loaded, you can print the total number of days that sales exceeded $1000.00 with the following code:

```
CTR = 0
FOR I = 1 TO 7
    IF  SALES(I) > 1000 THEN
        CTR = CTR + 1
    END IF            'Used with QBASIC
NEXT I
PRINT "Total No. of Days with Sales > 1000 is "; CTR
```

Self-Test

Consider these instructions:

```
INPUT VAR1
INPUT VAR2
INPUT VAR3
INPUT VAR4
INPUT VAR5
```

1. An array could be used in place of defining each variable separately because ____.
2. Suppose VAR3 and VAR5 were defined as VAR3$ and VAR5$, that is, as string variables. Could one array be used to define the five variables? Explain your answer.
3. Recode the instructions using an array to define the variables and inputting five numeric variables into VAR1 through VAR5.
4. Suppose you establish an array that contains 24 hourly temperatures for a given day. You could code the DIM statement for the array as DIM TEMP(24), which would allow you to access elements ____ through ____, although you would use elements ____ through ____.
5. The numbers in parentheses in the above are called ____.

   Assume the following array is in storage:

   > DIM TEMP(24)
   > TEMP(1) has the temperature for 1 AM, TEMP(2) has the temperature for 2 AM, and so on.

6. Write a routine to find the average temperature for the day.
7. Write a routine to find the lowest temperature for the day.
8. Write a routine to print the time when the temperature was the lowest.
9. Write a routine to find the number of hours in the day when the temperature fell below 20°.

Solutions

1. An array, defined properly, reserves the same amount of storage space for all variables as if each were defined individually. Also, each array element can be accessed just as if it were a separate variable.
2. No. When an array is defined, it must contain either all string or all numeric elements.
3. Code:

```
DIM VAR(5)
FOR I = 1 TO 5
    INPUT VAR(I)
NEXT I
END
```

4. TEMP(0); TEMP(24); TEMP(1); TEMP(24)
5. subscripts
6. Routine:

```
TOTAL = 0
FOR I = 1 TO 24
    TOTAL = TOTAL + TEMP(I)
NEXT I
AVERAGE = TOTAL / 24
PRINT "The average temperature was "; AVERAGE
```

7. Routine:

```
LOW.TEMP = 999
FOR I = 1 TO 24
    IF  TEMP(I) < LOW.TEMP THEN      'Press Ctrl+End for BASICA
        LOW.TEMP = Temp(I)
    END IF                   'Used with QBASIC
NEXT I
PRINT "The low for the day was "; LOW.TEMP
```

8. Routine:

```
LOW.TIME = 0
LOW.TEMP = 999
FOR I = 1 TO 24
    IF  TEMP(I) < LOW.TEMP THEN
        LOW.TEMP = TEMP(I)
        LOW.TIME = I
    END IF              'Used with QBASIC
NEXT I
PRINT "At "; LOW.TIME; ":00 the temperature was "; LOW.TEMP
```

9. Routine:

```
COUNT = 0
FOR I = 1 TO 24
    IF  TEMP(I) < 20 THEN
        COUNT = COUNT + 1
NEXT I
PRINT "The temperature fell below 20 "; COUNT;" hours"
```

Summary

I. Overview
   A. Data Organization
      1. Data that changes value during the execution of a program is known as variable data. It includes data entered as input, totals, and counters.

2. Data that maintains the same value throughout the program is known as constant or literal data.
3. Data may be numeric or string. Numeric variable names consist of letters and digits and begin with a letter. String variable names are similar to numeric variable names, except that they must end with a $. A numeric variable may contain digits, a decimal point, and a leading sign. A string variable can contain any character.

B. BASIC Input and Output Statements
1. The INPUT statement is used to enter data from the keyboard.
2. The LPRINT statement causes output to be sent to the printer, and the PRINT statement causes output to be displayed on the screen.
3. A comment line may be designated by using the REM statement or by beginning any line with a single quote ('). Comments may also be added to any statement with the use of the single quote:

```
T = 15.3      '15.3 is the value in T
```

C. Performing Arithmetic Operations
1. A numeric variable is specified to the left of the equal sign in an assignment statement (for example, LET TOTAL = . . . or TOTAL = . . .).
2. All arithmetic operations are specified to the right of the equal sign.
3. The order of evaluation of arithmetic operations is as follows.

^	Exponentiation
* or /	Multiply or divide
+ or −	Add or subtract

All operations on the same level are performed in sequence from left to right. *Note:* Parentheses ( ) override normal hierarchy rules.

II. Using Simple Relationals
A. Relations
IF a variable or literal is $<$, $>$, $=$, $<=$, $>=$, or $<>$ a second variable or literal, THEN a series of instructions is performed.

B. Comparisons
1. Numeric operands are compared algebraically.

$$12.0 = 12.00 = 12 = +12$$

2. String operands should contain the same number of characters for a logical comparison.
   a. "ABC" is equal to "ABC" only if both variables are the same length. Note that " ABC" $<$ " ABC" $<$ "ABC". (To store " ABC" or " ABC" in a string variable, you must use an assignment statement or input it with quotation marks as " ABC".)
   b. Shorter string operands are considered "less than" longer ones if all characters up to the length of the shorter field are equal. That is, "ABC" $<$ "ABC " $<$ "ABC " $<$ "ABCD".

3. The collating sequence used with most micros is called ASCII. With ASCII, numbers are less than letters. Also, uppercase letters are less than lowercase letters. That is, numbers are always compared correctly (0 < 1 < 2 . . .), uppercase letters are compared correctly ("A" < "B" < "C" . . .), and lowercase letters are also compared correctly ("a" < "b" < "c" . . .). But keep in mind that 0 < 1 . . . < 9 < "A" . . . < "Z" < "a" . . . < "z".

C. Compound Conditionals
 1. Format

IF (condition-1) OR (condition-2) THEN . . .
IF (condition-1) AND (condition-2) THEN . . .

 2. Hierarchy
    a. If ORs and ANDs are used in the same statement, ANDs are evaluated first from left to right, followed by ORs.
    b. Parentheses can be used to override this hierarchy rule.
III. The Four Logical Constructs
 A. Sequence
   Program steps are executed in the order they appear.
 B. Selection
   An IF-THEN-ELSE selects the instruction or instructions to be executed, depending on whether a condition is met.
 C. Iteration
   A series of steps is executed repeatedly, based on whether a given condition or conditions are met.
 D. Case
   One of a number of steps will be executed, depending on the contents of a variable or variables.
IV. Iterative Techniques
 A. A WHILE . . . WEND may be used to accomplish iteration.
   1. The loop is repeated until the condition is no longer met.
   2. If the condition is not met initially, the loop will never be executed, because the test is performed before the first execution of the loop.
 B. All forms of iteration can be nested.
V. FOR . . . NEXT Statements
 A. The FOR . . . NEXT statement is used when you want to perform a loop a predefined number of times in which a variable needs to be incremented (or decremented) by the same amount each time the loop is repeated.
 B. The FOR . . . NEXT accomplishes the following:
   1. Establishes and initializes a variable.
   2. Increments (or decrements) the variable.
   3. Specifies the range in which the variable is to vary.
VI. Subroutines for Top-Down Modular Programming
 A. A module, or subroutine, is a set of instructions that functions as a unit and performs a specific set of operations.

B. Subroutines minimize duplication of effort.

C. A GOSUB statement causes execution of a separate routine and then returns control to the statement following the GOSUB.

D. Subroutines are coded after the END statement.

E. Each subroutine is terminated by a RETURN that is coded on a line by itself.

F. Subroutines implement top-down modular design.

G. A subroutine is identified by a line number in BASICA and by a module name in QBASIC. In the BASICA instruction GOSUB 1000, for example, 1000 is a line number. In the QBASIC instruction GOSUB ErrorRoutine, ErrorRoutine is a module name.

H. GOSUB statements may be nested.

VII. Arrays are used to store a series of variables, all with the same format.

Key Terms

Alphanumeric variable	Iteration	Sentinel value
Array	Literal	Sequence
Case	Logical control construct	String constant
Collating sequence	Loop	String variable
Command	Module	Structured programming
Compound conditional	Nested conditional	Subroutine
Conditional statement	Nested iteration	Subscript
Constant	Nested while	Top-down programming
Editing	Numeric variable	Trailer
Format	Output	Variable
IF-THEN-ELSE	Prompt	
Input	Selection	

Final Quizzes
Self-test

1. What, if anything, is wrong with the following statement?

$$IF\ A = B\ OR\ IF\ A = C\ THEN$$
$$PRINT\ "A\ OK"$$

2. What, if anything, is wrong with the following statement?

$$IF\ A < 21\ OR\ A = 21\ AND\ A = 5\ OR\ A > 5\ THEN$$
$$PRINT\ "A\ OK"$$

3. The hierarchy rule for evaluating compound conditionals states that conditions surrounding the word _____ are evaluated first, followed by the conditions surrounding the word _____.

4. Write a single statement to print "A OK" if A is between 3 and 13, inclusive of the endpoints.

5. Write a single statement to print "A OK" if A is between 3 and 13, exclusive of the endpoints.
6. (T or F) A loop should be used whenever one set of instructions is to be executed when a condition is true and another set is to be executed when the condition is false.
7. (T or F) All subroutines should be coded after the END statement.
8. (T or F) A subroutine may be referenced from only one place in a program.

Identify the errors in the FOR statements in 9 and 10.
9. FOR CTR = 1 TO 4 STEP −1
10. FOR NAME$ = 1 TO 10
11. What will happen if the counter or variable in a loop is not modified?
12. Why is it best to use a top-down modular approach to designing and coding programs?

Solutions

1. The word IF should appear only once.
2. There should be parentheses around the conditions to make the statement logical: IF (A < 21 OR A = 21) AND (A = 5 OR A > 5)
3. AND; OR
4. IF A <= 13 AND A >= 3 THEN
       PRINT "A OK"
    END IF
5. IF A > 3 AND A < 13 THEN
       PRINT "A OK"
    END IF
6. F—A loop is coded when a section of code is to be executed repeatedly.
7. T
8. F—A subroutine may be referenced from more than one location in the program.
9. The STEP must specify a positive increment since CTR begins at 1 and ends at 4.
10. The counter variable must be numeric.
11. If the counter loop is not modified, the loop will repeat indefinitely (an infinite loop) because the loop condition will never be met.
12. A top-down modular approach makes it easier to debug and modify code. In addition, it leads to better designed programs.

True-False Questions

1. (T or F) A BASIC program that compiles without any errors will always run properly.
2. (T or F) BASIC programs must be converted into machine language before execution can occur.
3. (T or F) A comment in BASIC programs begins with REM or with an apostrophe (single-quote mark).

4. (T or F) Instructions are typically executed in sequence unless a WHILE . . . WEND or other logical control structure alters the flow.

5. (T or F) A trailer value is used to indicate that there is no more data to be processed.

6. (T or F) The LPRINT instruction is used to display data on a screen.

7. (T or F) The IF statement is used to implement the iteration control structure.

8. (T or F) An ELSE clause is a required part of the IF statement.

9. (T or F) A string variable cannot be compared to a numeric variable in a conditional.

10. (T or F) When an IF statement includes both an AND and an OR, the conditions surrounding the AND are evaluated first.

Practice Program

Write a program (1) without subroutines and (2) using subroutines to print the class average of a final exam for each of 10 classes. Each class has exactly 20 students, and each student has taken the exam. Thus 200 exam grades will be entered. Assume that the first 20 grades are for students in Class 1, the next 20 are for students in Class 2, and so on.

In QBASIC Without Subroutines:

```
'****************************************************************
' This program calculates the class average for 10 classes
' each with 20 students in it - no subroutines
'****************************************************************
LET CLASSCTR = 1
WHILE CLASSCTR <= 10
    LET STUDNO = 1
    LET TOTAL = 0
    WHILE STUDNO <= 20
        INPUT EXAM
        LET TOTAL = TOTAL + EXAM
        LET STUDNO = STUDNO + 1
    WEND
    LET AVERAGE = TOTAL / 20
    PRINT "Class Average for Class "; CLASSCTR; " is "; AVERAGE
    CLASSCTR = CLASSCTR + 1
WEND
END
```

In QBASIC With Subroutines:

```
'****************************************************************
' This program prints a class average for 10 classes with
' 20 students per class
```

```
'
'
' We do not need an initial read because we know precisely
' how many variables we will be processing
'*******************************************************************
LET CLASSCTR = 0
WHILE CLASSCTR < 10
    GOSUB INITIALIZE
    WHILE STUDNO < 20
        GOSUB SUB2
    WEND
    GOSUB AVERAGE
WEND
PRINT "End of Job"
END
'Subroutines go here
INITIALIZE:
    LET STUDNO = 0
    LET TOTAL = 0
RETURN
SUB2:
    INPUT EXAM
    LET TOTAL = TOTAL + EXAM
    LET STUDNO = STUDNO + 1
RETURN
AVERAGE:
    LET CLASSCTR = CLASSCTR + 1
    LET AVERAGE = TOTAL / 20
    PRINT "Class Average for Class "; CLASSCTR; " is"; AVERAGE
RETURN
```

Programming Assignments

1. A company pays its 15 salespeople (numbered 01 through 15) a monthly salary of $2500 plus a 2 percent commission. Write a program to input Salesperson Number and Amount Sold and calculate and print the Amount Sold and the Salary Plus Commission for each salesperson.
2. Print a table that will show the square and square root of all integer numbers between 1 and 100. Note that no input is required.
3. Write a program to calculate the Social Security tax, where a variable called SALARY is entered as data. Assume that Social Security tax is equal to 6.2 percent of SALARY up to $55,500. Salary in excess of $55,500 is not taxed.
4. Doughnuts cost $0.25 each if a customer purchases less than a dozen. The doughnuts are $0.18 each if 12 or more are purchased. Write a program to read in the number of doughnuts purchased and calculate the total price. The pro-

gram should be able to operate on a variable number of input lines entered. Plan the program first with pseudocode.

5. A school cafeteria charges $0.60 for a cup of coffee that costs it $0.29 if less than 100 cups are sold in a day and $0.24 if it sells 100 or more cups in a day. Write a program to input the number of cups sold per day and to print the profit made each day. Plan the program first with pseudocode.

Appendix A

Reserved Words in QBASIC and BASICA

Words with no asterisk (*) are reserved in both QBASIC and BASICA. Words with one asterisk (*) are QBASIC only reserved words. Words with two asterisks (**) are BASICA only reserved words. Remember, these words cannot be used as variable names.

ABS	*CLNG	DEFINT
ABSOLUTE	CLOSE	*DEFLNG
ACCESS	CLS	DEFSNG
AND	COLOR	*DEFSTR
ANY	COM	**DELETE
APPEND	COMMON	DIM
AS	**CONT	*DO . . . LOOP
ASC	*CONST	*DOUBLE
ATN	COS	DRAW
**AUTO	CSNG	*$DYNAMIC
*BASE	CSRLIN	**EDIT
BEEP	CVD	ELSE
BLOAD	*CVDMBF	*ELSEIF
BSAVE	CVI	END
CALL	*CVL	ENVIRON
*CALL ABSOLUTE	CVS	ENVIRON$
*CASE	*CVSMBF	EOF
CDBL	DATA	EQV
CHAIN	DATE$	ERASE
*CHDIR	*DECLARE	ERDEV
CHR$	**DEF	ERDEV$
CINT	*DEF FN	ERL
CIRCLE	*DEF SEG	ERR
CLEAR	DEFDBL	ERROR

129

*EXIT	LOG	*PMAP
EXP	*LONG	POINT
FIELD	*LOOP	POKE
*FILEATTR	LPOS	POS
FILES	LPRINT	PRESET
FIX	*LPRINT USING	PRINT
**FNxxxxxxxx	LSET	*PRINT USING
*FOR	*LTRIM$	**PRINT#
**FOR . . . NEXT	**MERGE	PSET
FRE	MID$	PUT
*FREEFILE	MKDIR	*RANDOM
*FUNCTION	MKD$	RANDOMIZE
GET	*MKDMBF$	READ
GOSUB	MKI$	*REDIM
GOTO	*MKL$	REM
HEX$	MKS$	**RENUM
**IF	*MKSMBF$	RESET
*IF . . . THEN . . . ELSE	MOD	RESTORE
IMP	**MOTOR	RESUME
INKEY$	NAME	RETURN
INP	**NEW	RIGHT$
INPUT	NEXT	RMDIR
**INPUT#	NOT	RND
INPUT$	OCT$	RSET
**INSTR	OFF	*RTRIM$
INT	*ON	RUN
*INTEGER	*ON COM	**SAVE
*IOCTL	*ON ERROR	SCREEN
*IOCTL$	*ON . . . GOSUB	*SEEK
*IS	*ON PEN	*SELECT CASE
KEY	*ON PLAY	SGN
**KEY$	*ON STRIG	*SHARED
KILL	*ON TIMER	SHELL
*LBOUND	OPEN	SIN
*LCASE$	*OPEN COM	*SINGLE
LEFT$	**OPTION	*SLEEP
LEN	*OPTION BASE	SOUND
LET	OR	SPACE$
LINE	OUT	*SPC
*LINE INPUT	*OUTPUT	**SPCI
LIST	PAINT	SQR
**LLIST	*PALETTE	*STATIC
**LOAD	*PCOPY	*$STATIC
LOC	PEEK	STEP
LOCATE	PEN	STICK
LOF	PLAY	STOP

STR$	TROFF	VIEW
STRIG	TRON	*VIEW PRINT
*STRING	*TYPE	WAIT
STRING$	*UNBOUND	WEND
*SUB	*UCASE	**WHILE
SWAP	*UNLOCK	*WHILE . . . WEND
SYSTEM	*UNTIL	WIDTH
TAB	USING	WINDOW
TAN	**USR	WRITE
THEN	*VAL	**WRITE#
TIME$	*VARPTR	XOR
TIMER	VARPTR$	
TO	*VARSEG	

Appendix B

Brief Introduction to QBASIC and QuickBASIC Menus

This appendix is an overview of QBASIC and QuickBASIC that you can use for quick reference. Features not covered previously in this text are presented to provide a more complete introduction to these versions of the BASIC language. Note that QBASIC is very similar to QuickBASIC—many of the commands are identical.

QuickBASIC Features

To load the QuickBASIC compiler, place the disk with QB.EXE in the A or C drive, depending on your system, and type QB. Depending on which version you have, your main screen display will appear similar to Figure B.1.

The QuickBASIC commands appear on the top of the screen. To use one of them, hold down the Alt key and press the first letter of the desired command. Pressing the Shift plus F1 keys at any point provides context-sensitive help. Note the high degree of commonality between QBASIC and QuickBASIC.

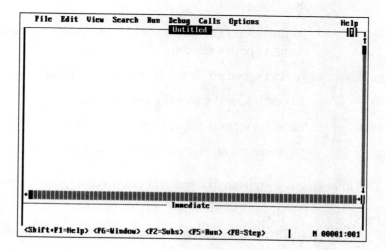

Figure B.1
QuickBASIC main screen display.

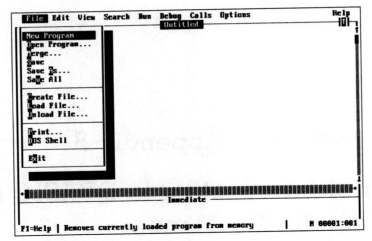

Figure B.2
QuickBASIC File
command pull-
down menu.

When you select a command, you will see a pull-down menu from which you can make additional selections. Figure B.2 illustrates the pull-down menu for the File command. You may use the ↓ or ↑ cursor and then press the Enter key to select an item from a pull-down menu, or you can key in the highlighted letter from the pull-down menu.

Pull-down menu items that end with three dots (. . .) will, when selected, display a dialog box requesting user information. For example, Alt + F(ile), then L(oad) File . . . requires you to key in some data, in this case a file name. A dialog box would then be displayed requesting you to enter the name of the file to be loaded in. See Figure B.3 for an illustration of a dialog box.

The following is a brief summary of QBASIC and QuickBASIC commands:

Command	**Use**
File	To load, save, or define a program file
Edit	To alter a program file by moving, deleting, or copying portions of the text
View	To display various segments of a program or to display and/or change options selected
Search	To find specified elements in a program and/or change them
Run	To compile and execute a program
Debug	To select various debugging aids when testing a program
Calls	To reference other modules in a program—only with QBASIC

The following is a summary of special keys used in QBASIC and QuickBASIC:

Key(s)	**Use**
F1 function key	To display context-sensitive help
Ctrl + Y	To delete a line at the cursor

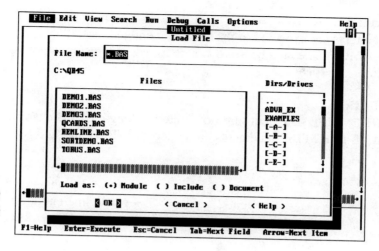

Figure B.3
QuickBASIC dialog box.

Home	To go to the beginning of a program line
End	To go to the end of a program line

The following is a list of global cursor moves:

Key(s)	Use
PgDn or Page Down	Scrolls a full page down
PgUp or Page Up	Scrolls a full page up
Ctrl + Home	Cursor moves to the beginning of the file
Ctrl + End	Cursor moves to the end of the file
Ctrl + →	Cursor moves to the beginning of the next word
Ctrl + ←	Cursor moves to the beginning of the previous word

The following is a list of special commands:

Key(s)	Use
Alt + F(ile), P(rint . . .)	To print part or all of a currently loaded program
Ctrl + F10	To eliminate the Immediate window from the QuickBASIC Screen (Ctrl + F10 is a toggle switch)
Alt + R(un) (then Enter or Shift + F5 key)	To run an existing program

Logical Control Constructs in QBASIC and QuickBASIC

Like all programming languages, QBASIC and QuickBASIC have four logical control constructs: sequence, selection, iteration, and case structure.

Sequence

Statements are executed in the sequence entered, not in line number sequence as in BASICA. Line numbers are not required; we recommend that you eliminate them.

Selection

IF-THEN-ELSE statements are not limited in length to 255 characters as with BASICA. IF-THEN-ELSE statements are coded as follows and end with END IF.

```
IF condition THEN
      statement-1          Each can be on a
      statement-2          separate line ended by
          .                pressing the Enter key
          .
          .

  ELSE
      statement-3          Each can be on a
      statement-4          separate line ended by
          .                pressing the Enter key
          .
          .

  END IF                   The IF block ends with
                           an END IF similar to
                           ENDIF in pseudocode
```

Iteration

WHILE . . . WEND and FOR . . . NEXT are permitted as with BASICA. You may also use a DO WHILE . . . LOOP in place of WHILE . . . WEND or you may use a DO UNTIL . . . LOOP. The following sets of code are equivalent.

```
DO WHILE CTR <= 20       DO UNTIL CTR > 20
    .                        .
    .                        .
    .                        .
LOOP                     LOOP
```

Case Structure

In place of ON GOSUB, you use SELECT CASE . . . END SELECT with GOSUBs. A GOSUB label can be used in place of GOSUB line numbers.

Example

```
INPUT MENU.ITEM
SELECT CASE MENU.ITEM
    CASE 1
        GOSUB SALARY.CHANGE      'Labels may be used with GOSUBs
```

```
    CASE 2
        GOSUB NAME.CHANGE
    CASE 3
        GOSUB ADDRESS.CHANGE
    CASE 4
        GOSUB DEPT.CHANGE
    CASE ELSE
        PRINT "ERROR"
END SELECT
```

Procedures

QuickBASIC permits separate modules to be coded in which the programmer can control the data passed from the main program to the procedure and back again.

Arrays

DIM EXAM(1:20) can be used to establish a 20-element array, which is referenced as EXAM(1) through EXAM(20).

Debugging

The following debugging options are available with QBASIC and QuickBASIC using the Debug command.

1. The Trace feature allows you to step through the program as it is executed, one line at a time.

   - Press F8 to manually step through a program.

   - Select the Trace On option of the Debug command to automatically step through a program as each line is executed.

   - Use the TRON instruction within the program itself to trace a program or segment when the instruction is encountered. (TROFF is an instruction that terminates tracing.)

2. Another feature enables you to display the contents of variables as a program is traced or executed. Select the Add Watch option of the Debug command and then enter variables to be watched. These variables will be displayed above the program, and their values will change as the program is traced or executed.

3. When a portion of a program functions properly or need not be tested at some point during debugging, you may want to bypass it. Preface such instructions with a single quote or apostrophe so that the compiler treats them as comments.

4. To select a breakpoint [a line(s) or instruction(s) at which you wish to suspend program execution so that you can analyze results or variables selected by the Add Watch option], move the cursor to the instruction to serve as a breakpoint. Then press the F9 function key or select the Toggle Breakpoint option of the Debug command [Alt-D(ebug), B(reakpoint)]. The instruction selected will be

highlighted. When the instruction is to be executed, the program is suspended. To clear the breakpoint, select the Clear All Breakpoints option of the Debug command.

The QuickBASIC Environment

The following outline summarizes how you interact with your computer while working in QuickBASIC. Letters in boldface type (e.g., **A**) mean that you press that key or enter that letter.

I. Customizing the QuickBASIC or QBASIC Screen
   A. Use Alt + **V**(iew), **O**(ptions) in QuickBASIC or Alt + **O**(ptions) + **D**(isplay) in QBASIC.
   B. By using the cursor arrow keys, you can set foreground and background colors for the following elements.
      1. **N**ormal Text
      2. **C**urrent Statement (the statement being traced)
      3. **B**reakpoint Lines
   C. You can set a highlight for each of the above; **C**urrent Statement and **B**reakpoint Lines can also be set for **B**link or **U**nderline.
   D. **S**croll Bars
      1. Use the scroll bars to size a screen with a mouse.
      2. The default is to set scroll bars on, but they can be set off if you are not using a mouse.
   E. **T**ab Stops
      1. The default for indentation is eight characters when the Tab key is pressed.
      2. You can change it to any number.
   F. Setting Options in the Dialog Box
      1. To move from option to option, use the Tab key.
      2. To change a color, use the cursor arrows when at the required option.
      3. To change highlighting, use the space bar when at the required option.
      4. To omit scroll bars, use the space bar.
      5. To return to previous lines or to skip lines, enter the highlighted letter.
      6. Press Enter to store changes; press Esc to cancel changes.
II. Working with the Immediate Window (available with QBASIC as well)
   A. Use this window for executing from 1 to 10 instructions immediately.
   B. To adjust the size of the Immediate Window
      1. Press Alt + (plus key) to increase the size one line at a time.
      2. Press Ctrl + F10 to increase the size of the window to the full screen. Ctrl and F10 are toggle keys.
III. Creating Executable Files—QuickBASIC Only
   A. An executable file is a debugged program file in machine language that does not require the QuickBASIC editor and compiler for loading and translating. That is, it can be run directly from DOS.
   B. Press Alt-**R**(un), **X** for Make E**X**E file to create such a file.

C. To run the program, type the program name from DOS.
D. The following QuickBASIC files are required to create an executable file.

BC.EXE   LINK.EXE   BRUN40.LIB   BCOM40.LIB

IV. Saving Files
A. You can save QuickBASIC files in QuickBASIC form, only readable by the QuickBASIC system, or in a format readable by other BASIC compilers. When you type Alt + **F**(ile), **S**(ave), the computer enables you to specify the format in which you want the file saved. Use the Tab key to select a format. The default is to save the file in QuickBASIC form.
B. After working on a program and saving it, select Alt + **F**(ile), **N**(ew) Program before loading in a new program.

V. Using the Edit Menu
A. QuickBASIC only: If you make a change to a previously entered program line, you can undo the change by pressing Alt + **E**(dit), **U**(ndo) or Alt + Backspace while the cursor is on the designated line.
B. To move and copy blocks of instructions, use Shift + → to designate characters as part of a block of text or Shift + ↓ to designate a line as part of a block of text.
C. To move a block of text, designate the block, select Alt + **E**(dit), (Cu)**t** to delete the text; then move the cursor to the desired point and press Alt + **E**(dit), **P**(aste) to move it.
D. To copy a block of text, designate the block, select Alt + **E**(dit), **C**(opy); move the cursor to the desired position; then press Alt + **E**(dit), **P**(aste) to copy it.
E. To delete a block of text, designate the block, press Alt + **E**(dit), (Cu)**t** to delete it temporarily and Alt + **E**(dit), (Cl)**e**(ar) to delete it permanently.

IV. Using the Search Command
A. To find and/or change elements in a program, use the Search command.
B. You can make changes globally, or you can verify each change before it is made.

VII. Using a Mouse
You can use a mouse in place of a keyboard for pointing to elements in a dialog box and selecting required entries.

VIII. You can size screens by using a mouse or by pressing Alt + + (plus key) or Alt + − (minus key).

Index

A

Alphanumeric data, 18
AND, in compound conditional, 80, 81
Apostrophe ('), 11
Arithmetic operations
   counters, incrementing, 43
   hierarchy of, 40–42
   operators for, 18, 36
   running totals, 43–44
   sample program, 38–39
Arrays
   accessing with subscript, 115–116
   coding guidelines, 117
   defining size, DIM statement, 114–115
   FOR...NEXT for processing of, 116–117
   functions of, 113
   QuickBASIC and QBASIC, 137
   reading data into, 118
   to store series of data elements, 113–114
ASCII computers, collating sequence,
   71–72
Assignment statement, 36–38
   coding guidelines, 45
   format of, 36
   operators used with, 36
   sample program with arithmetic
     operations, 38–39
   valid and invalid statements, examples
     of, 37–38
Asterisk (*), 17, 37–38

B

Backspace key, 20
BASIC
   accessing on system, 19
   development of, 1
   entering and running program using
     different translator or program, 24–25

program writing, steps in, 3–8
   versions of, 1–2, 19
BASICA, 1, 2
   accessing on system, 20
   deleting instruction line, 21
   error correction in, 20–21
   execution sequence, 10
   GOSUB, 103–105, 107–109
   IF–THEN–ELSE, 61–66, 75–76, 79–80
   inserting instruction line, 21
   line numbering, 8–9, 10, 17
   reserved words for, 129–131
   system commands, 21–22
   WHILE...WEND, 136
Brackets ([ ]), 46–47
Breakpoints, 137–138

C

CALLS, 134
Caret ($^\wedge$), 37
Case conventions, 10, 17
Case sensitivity
   alphanumeric comparison and, 71–72
   and insensitivity, 10, 33
Case structure
   coding with, 108–109
   function of, 59, 87
   ON–GOSUB, 59, 108–109
   QBASIC, 136–137
   QuickBASIC, 136–137
   SELECT CASE...END SELECT, 136
Coding guidelines, 10, 45, 47–48, 110, 115,
   117
Collating sequence, 71–72
Comma (,), 34, 47, 53–54
Comment lines, 11
Comments, 11, 17
   nature of, 17

141